Slow Cooker Cookbook for Beg

GH00391307

Rediscover the Joy of Simmering Delicious, ... Cost Recipes in the Morning and Finding Them Ready When You Get Home

TABLE OF CONTENTS

1 INTRODUCTION

1.1 What is a slow cooker?

The term "slow cooker" refers to any electric device with a glazed ceramic pot or crock. The phrases "Slow cooker" and "CrockPot" are generally interchangeable since the first company to develop a slow cooker (Competitor) named their product Crock-Pot®. Slow cookers come in a variety of capacities now, ranging from 1 to 12 quarts. Slow cookers require extended cooking periods, low cooking temperatures, and moisture produced by a tight-fitting cover to keep heat in and cook food. Slow cookers produce a slow simmer when put on a low setting temperature between 180–200°F. The high setting cooks food roughly 2-2 ½ times faster than the low setting and has a temperature range of 280–300°F. A slow cooker's major benefit is convenience, even if cooking time might range from 4 to 15 hours.

1.2 What's the operation to use a slow cooker?

When using a slow cooker, the chef adds raw food and either preheated liquid or a liquid like stock, wine, or water to the appliance. The slow cooker is covered and turned on. The crock and lid completely cover the contents, allowing them to maintain a constant temperature. At this temperature, vapors are created, which condense on the bottom of the cover and turn back into liquid, leaching certain water-soluble vitamins. The liquid also disperses tastes while transferring heat from the pot's sides to the contents. It takes 15 to 20 minutes to restore the warmth and steam if the lid is removed while cooking. Therefore, if the cover is taken off while cooking, a longer cooking time and additional liquid will be needed. Basic slow cookers must be manually turned on and off since they only provide low, medium, high, or warm settings. Modern slow cookers contain computerized timing devices that allow a cook to configure the slow cooker to set out several functions (For example, warm followed by one hour of high and one hour of low temperature). Safe internal temperatures for meats include 145°F for whole cuts of the beef, pig, and lamb with a 3-minute resting period, 165°F for poultry, and 160°F for ground beef, pork, and lamb.

1.3 What are the advantages and disadvantages of a slow cooker?

Advantages
- Slow cookers are budget friendly
- Slow cookers spare your time.
- The slow cooker requires little supervision.
- Energy-efficient
- The slow cooker adds flavors to foods.
- Meat becomes more tender in the slow cooker.
- Nutrients remain intact during cooking in the slow cooker.
- It is easy to operate a slow cooker.

Disadvantages
- The cooking speed is low.
- Slow cooking doesn't suit impromptu changes.
- Not every recipe works well in a slow cooker.
- Slow cookers require pre-planning for cooking.

- A slow cooker may cause uneven cooking.
- Slow cookers can't be used for searing.

1.4 What are the foods that should not be cooked in a slow cooker and why?

Even though a slow cooker is a multipurpose kitchen appliance, not everything can be prepared in it. The list of items you shouldn't cook in a slow cooker is provided below.

Raw meat

The low temperature of a slow cooker doesn't allow the meat to brown. Don't add the meat without browning it in the slow cooker if you don't like a bland stew.

Lean cuts of meat

Lean cuts of meat, such as chicken breast, pig fillet, and fillet steak, cook down to tough leather whereas harder, sinewy pieces of meat, such as beef shin, oxtail, and hog shoulder, become soft morsels when cooked slowly. Leave such meat parts for frying or grilling instead.

Meat with skin

A dry heat source like a grill or oven is necessary for skin-on meat to crisp up. if you cook them in the slow cooker, it will lead to unpleasant, flubbed chunks of skin in the stew.

Dried Legumes seeds and beans

A slow cooker seems like a fantastic solution as dried beans need to soak for at least an overnight before cooking. The main issue is that some beans, especially kidney beans, have a naturally present toxin which eliminates in the slow cooker. The temperature needed to eliminate that poison (212 °F) is rarely reached by slow cookers. Before adding seeds and beans to a slow cooker, they should always be soaked, washed, and cooked for at least 10 minutes.

Dairy and dairy products

Dairy products separate when cooked for an extended time. A gritty, watery mess is certain if yogurt, milk, or cream, is added to the slow cooker at the start of cooking. stir it in when the food is cooked.

Soft and delicate vegetables

Long-time cooking is best for hard root vegetables but not for soft or delicate vegetables (Peas, Asparagus, etc.) as it will turn them into mushy pulp.

Seafood

Seafood needs a short time to be cooked, so it will be destroyed if cooked for a long time. Octopuses and squid are the only exceptions; they need slow cooking to perfectly tenderize them.

Excessive liquid

Slow cookers are great at keeping moisture inside, so adding too much water or broth will result in a bland dish. If you're using a simmer recipe that wasn't intended to be made in a slow cooker, cut the liquid amount to half.

1.5   Food list

Permitted Foods	Foods to Avoid
Whole chicken, chicken thighs (pick the right cut), and chicken teriyaki	Any kind of pasta and spaghetti
Tough cuts of beef (short ribs, stew meat, grounded beef, and chuck roast)	Long grain rice
Pork (pork ribs, butt, shoulder, and ham)	Any kind of frozen foods (frozen meat like chicken or beef and vegetables)
Minced meat, ground turkey, octopus, and sausages	Seafood like fish, shellfish, oysters, and bacon
Steaks, chilis, stews, and broths	Fresh, soft herbs and delicate vegetables like (Zucchini, peas, tomatoes, spinach, and asparagus)
Any kind of dip (any vegetable dip like onion, garlic, and chives) Sauces (apple and cranberry sauce)	Any kind of dried beans (white, green, red, or kidney beans)
Vegetables (boiled or roasted), lentils, and wild rice	Milk, eggs, and cheese (like any kind of dessert)
Bread dough, ham, and casseroles	Lean, raw, or boneless white meat poultry
Chicken, mutton, beef, or any vegetable soups and meatballs	Any kind of wine and alcohol

2   SHOPPING LIST FOR A WEEK OF DIET

Quantity	Quantity in gram
1 ½ pound pork ribs	679gram pork ribs
3 ounces can tomato paste	85gram can of tomato paste
½ cup honey	170gram honey
2 pounds baby back ribs	907gram baby back ribs
1 bottle of barbecue sauce	510gram bottle barbecue sauce
1 whole chicken	1814gram whole chicken
5 medium onion	750gram onion
2 large stalks of celery	128gram stalk celery
3 pounds chicken thigh	1360gram chicken thigh
1-ounce fresh ginger	28gram fresh ginger
4 pounds of mixed beef	1814gram of mixed beef
4 medium carrots	400gram carrots
12 small eggs	456gram eggs
5-ounce potatoes	150gram potatoes
2-ounce Spanish sausage	56gram Spanish sausage
5 cups plain granola cereal	545gram plain granola cereal
1 cup oatmeal	80gram oatmeal
¼ cup sultanas	62.5gram sultanas
4tbsp. low-fat butter	56.7gram low-fat butter

3 MEASUREMENT CONVERSION CHART

Unlike UK recipes, which ask for metric measurements, US recipes usually measure ingredients in either pounds and ounces or cups and spoons.

With this helpful guide to weight and volume conversions, you can bake and prepare your favorite US recipes without having to make any guesses.

When following a recipe, choose one and stay with it rather than combining imperial and metric measurements.

3.1 Volume conversions for liquids

Imperial	US cups	Metric
1/2 fl Oz.	1 tablespoon	15ml
1 fl Oz	1/8 cup	30ml
2 fl Oz	1/4 cup	60ml
2 1/2 fl Oz	1/3 cup	80ml
4 fl Oz	1/2 cup	120ml
5 fl Oz	2/3 cup	160ml
6 fl Oz	3/4 cup	180ml
8 fl Oz	1 cup	240ml

Metric and US cups differ somewhat from one another. A US cup contains around 240ml of liquid compared to a regular metric cup's 250ml. This minor variation won't often have an impact on the outcome of a dish. In cases of uncertainty, convert US cups to metric milliliters.

3.2 Weight conversions for dry ingredients

Imperial	Metric	Imperial	Metric
1/4 Oz	7g	8 Oz	225g
1/2 Oz	15g	9 Oz	255g
1 Oz	30g	10 Oz	280g
2 Oz	60g	11 Oz	310g
3 Oz	85g	12 Oz	340g
4 Oz	110g	13 Oz	370g
5 Oz	140g	14 Oz	400g
6 Oz	170g	15 Oz	425g
7 Oz	200g	1 lb	450g

3.3 US cup measurements to grams conversion

In the US, cups are frequently used to measure ingredients. When measuring volume, cups are perfect, but it might be difficult to convert cup measurements to grams because the equivalent weight depends on the component. For instance, a cup of sugar weighs around 225g, but a cup of flour may only weigh 150g. The chart below provides an approximate conversion of several frequently used substances from US cup measurements to grams. However, it's often advisable to stick to the recipe's cup measurements. A set of measuring cups can be purchased online, in big supermarkets, department stores, or housewares shops.

US cups	Weight in grams
1 stick butter	113g
1 cup grated cheese	110g
1 cup uncooked rice	200g
1 cup ground almonds	110g
1 cup currants	150g
1 cup sultanas/raisins	200g
1 cup butter/margarine/lard	225g
1 cup icing sugar	125g
1 cup brown sugar	200g
1 cup caster/granulated sugar	225g
1 cup flour	150g

3.4 Oven temperatures

Most UK ovens only display temperatures in Celsius, but US recipes often provide oven temperatures in degrees Fahrenheit. Find the UK equivalent using the table below. Keep in mind to lower the temperature by 20 degrees in fan-assisted ovens as illustrated below.

Description	Electric °F	Electric °C	Electric °C Fan	Gas mark
Very hot	475	240	220	9
Very hot	450	230	210	8
Hot	425	220	200	7
Fairly hot	400	200	180	6
Moderately hot	375	190	170	5
Moderate	350	180	160	4
Warm	325	160	140	3
Cool	300	150	130	2
Cool	275	140	120	1
Very cool	250	120	100	1/2
Very cool	225	110	90	1/4

3.5 U.S. Standard to U.K. Measurement Conversions

U.S Standard	U.K
1 tablespoon	2 1/2 teaspoon
1/4 teaspoon	1/4 teaspoon (scant)
1/2 teaspoon	1/2 teaspoon (scant)
3/4 teaspoon	1/2 teaspoon (rounded)
1 teaspoon	3/4 teaspoon (slightly rounded)
5 cups	4 cups and 3 tablespoons
4 3/4 cups	3 3/4 cups and 3 tablespoons
4 2/3 cups	3 3/4 cups and 2 tablespoons
4 1/2 cups	3 3/4 cups
4 1/3 cups	3 1/2 cups and 2 tablespoons
4 1/4 cups	3 1/2 cups and 1 dessertspoon
4 cups	3 1/3 cups
3 3/4 cups	3 cups and 2 tablespoons
3 2/3 cups	3 cups and 1 tablespoon
3 1/2 cups	2 3/4 cups and 3 tablespoons
3 1/3 cups	2 3/4 cups
3 1/4 cups	2 2/3 cups and 1 dessertspoon
3 cups	2 1/2 cups
2 3/4 cups	2 1/4 cups and 1 dessertspoon
2 2/3 cups	2 1/4 cups
2 1/2 cups	2 cups and 2 dessertspoons
2 1/3 cups	1 3/4 cups and 3 tablespoons
2 1/4 cups	1 3/4 cups and 2 tablespoons
2 cups	1 2/3 cups
1 3/4 cups	1 1/3 cups and 2 tablespoons
1 2/3 cups	1 1/4 cups and 2 tablespoons
1 1/2 cups	1 1/4 cups
1 1/3 cups	1 cup and 2 tablespoons
1 1/4 cups	1 cup and 1 dessertspoon
1 cup	3/4 cup and 2 dessertspoons
3/4 cup	1/2 cup plus 2 tablespoons
2/3 cup	1/2 cup plus 1 tablespoon
1/2 cup	1/3 cup plus 2 dessertspoons
1/3 cup	1/4 cup plus 1 teaspoon
1/4 cup	1/4 cup plus 1 dessertspoon

4   BREAKFAST RECIPES

4.1   Slow cooker cinnamon oatmeal

8 Servings | Preparation time: 10 mins | Cook time: 180 mins

Ingredients/Food list

- Old-fashioned oats, 1 cup
- peeled and sliced tart apple
- Walnuts, ¼ cup
- Raisins, ½ cup
- Brown sugar, ¼ cup
- Salt, ¼ tsp.
- Cinnamon, ½ tsp.
- Butter, 1 tbsp.
- 2% milk, 2 cups

Preparation/Procedure

1. Spray the slow cooker with the melted butter.
2. Add oats, apple tart, brown sugar, raisins, and salt, and mix well.
3. Transfer the above mixture to the slow cooker.
4. Cook for 3 hours until it absorbs all the liquid and becomes soft after cooking.
5. After cooking let the oatmeal cool for a few minutes.
6. Serve with milk, walnuts, and cinnamon powder sprinkled on oatmeal.

Storage

Cover the container with a lid and store it in the refrigerator.

Reheating

It is not necessary, just keep it at room temperature for a few minutes.

Nutritional facts/values (per serving)

Calories: 340 | Fat: 13g | Carbohydrates: 32g | Protein: 10g | Sodium: 225mg | Potassium: 300mg | Sugar: 10g

4.2   Mexican omelet

4 Servings | Preparation time: 10 mins | Cook time: 160 mins

Ingredients/Food list

- Olive oil, 1 tsp.
- Peeled and sliced potatoes, 2 cups
- Chopped onions 1- ¼ cup
- Chopped bell peppers, 1 cup
- Brown sugar, ¼ cup
- Large eggs, 3
- Separate Egg whites, 6
- Salt, ¼ tsp.
- Black pepper, ¼ tsp.

Preparation/Procedure

1. Spray the slow cooker heavily with cooking spray.
2. Add olive oil, onions, potatoes, and bell pepper to a pan. Stir occasionally and cook until the potato just starts to brown, and the onion is soft.
3. Pour the above mixture into the slow cooker. Mix egg mixture by combining egg whites, black peppers, and salt. Overtop the cookers veggies with egg mixture. Close the lid and let it simmer at low temperature for 2.5 hours for the core to cook.
4. After it's done cut it into pieces and serve it with bread.

Storage

Cover the container with a lid and store it in the refrigerator.

Reheating

Reheat it in the pan or microwave it for 2 minutes.

Nutritional facts/values (per serving)

Calories: 193 | Fat: 6g | Carbohydrates: 21g | Protein: 12g | Sodium: 434mg | Potassium: 593mg | Sugar: 4g

4.3 Meatball sandwiches

6 Servings | Preparation time: 30 mins | Cook time: 260 mins

Ingredients/Food list

- Peeled eggplant, 1 small
- Grounded beef, 1-½ cups
- Grated cheese, ½ cup
- Breadcrumbs, ½ cup
- Large egg, 1
- Salt, 1 tsp.
- Seasoning of your choice, 2 tbsp.
- Bell peppers, 2 cups
- 1-½ cup pasta sauce
- Toasted buns, 6

Preparation/Procedure

1. Cook eggplant until it becomes soft in a pan with simmering water. Drain the water and mash the eggplant.
2. Combine eggplant with beef, cheese, salt, and seasoning. Shape it into balls and coat them with eggs and breadcrumbs.
3. Combine the meatballs with bell peppers and pasta sauce in the slow cooker.
4. Cook in the slow cooker for 4-5 hours at a low temperature.
5. Serve meatballs with sauce in each bun.

Storage

Cover the container with a lid and store it in the refrigerator.

Reheating

Reheat the leftovers in the microwave for 2 minutes.

Nutritional facts/values (per serving)

Calories: 565 | Fat: 20g | Carbohydrates: 70 | Protein: 40g | Sodium: 559mg | Potassium: 750mg | Sugar: 65g

4.4 Baked Apples with Stuffing

4 Servings | Preparation time: 20 mins | Cook time: 240 mins

Ingredients/Food list

- Medium green apples, 4
- Mixed dry fruit, chopped nicely, ½ cup
- Chopped and toasted pecans, ¼ cup
- Butter, 3 tbsp.
- Brown sugar, 3 tbsp.
- Cinnamon powder, ½ tsp.
- Nutmeg powder, ¼ tsp.

Preparation/Procedure

1. Peel the apples and remove the inner parts for filling.
2. Mix dry fruits, pecans, brown sugar, and butter in a bowl.
3. Fill the apples with the above mixture and transfer them to the slow cooker.
4. Cook in the slow cooker for 4 hours at low temperature or 2 hours at medium temperature.
5. Let the apples cool after cooking.
6. Serve by sprinkling cinnamon and nutmeg powder.

Storage

Cover the container with a lid and store it in the refrigerator.

Reheating

It is not necessary, just keep it at room temperature for a few minutes. If you want to reheat, use a microwave.

Nutritional facts/values (per serving)

Calories: 241 | Fat: 10g | Carbohydrates: 4 | Protein: 1g | Sodium: 37mg | Potassium: 150mg | Sugar: 28g

4.5 Sweet quinoa

8 Servings | Preparation time: 5-10 mins | Cook time: 360-480 mins

Ingredients/Food list

- Quinoa, 2 cups
- Filtered water, 4 cups
- Coconut milk, 2 cup
- Honey, 4 tbsp.
- Salt, ½ tsp.
- Cinnamon powder, 1 tsp.
- Any dry fruit, 1 tbsp.

Preparation/Procedure

1. Rinse the quinoa with fresh running water for a few minutes to clean it properly.
2. Add quinoa, coconut milk, salt, and honey and mix well.
3. Transfer the mixture to the slow cooker filled with 4 cups of water.
4. Cook in the slow cooker for 8 hours at a low temperature (overnight).
5. Serve with cinnamon powder and dry fruit coatings.

Storage

Cover the container with a lid and store it in the refrigerator for 1 week.

Reheating

Reheat in a pan or microwave it for 2 minutes and serve hot for a better taste.

Nutritional facts/values (per serving)

Calories: 330 | Fat: 15g | Carbohydrates: 40g | Protein: 7g | Sodium: 166mg | Potassium: 187mg | Sugar: 10g

4.6 Slow cooker baked potatoes

8 Servings | Preparation time: 10 mins | Cook time: 260 mins

Ingredients/Food list

- Small potatoes cut into cubes, 6 cups
- Red bell pepper cut into cubes, 1
- Green bell pepper cut into cubes, 1
- Minced garlic, 1 tbsp.
- Onion cut into cubes, ½ cup
- Roasted paprika, 2 tbsp.
- Salt, 2 tbsp.
- Butter and olive oil, 2 tbsp.

Preparation/Procedure

1. Spray the slow cooker with cooking spray.
2. Add potatoes, bell peppers, garlic, onions, salt, butter, and paprika. mix well and spread olive oil on top.
3. Cook in the slow cooker for 4-5 hours at a low temperature. The time and temperature may vary according to your slow cooker.
4. Serve hot with any sauce of your taste or olive oil.

Storage

Cover the container with a lid and store it in the refrigerator

Reheating

Microwave for 2-3 minutes and serve hot.

Nutritional facts/values (per serving)

Calories: 190 | Fat: 8g | Carbohydrates: 32g | Protein: 3g | Sodium: 641mg | Potassium: 535mg | Sugar: 2g

4.7 Slow cooker baked cinnamon rolls

10 Servings | Preparation time: 30 mins | Cook time: 210 mins

Ingredients/Food list

For dough

- All-purpose flour, 1-¾ cups
- Warm water, ¾ cups
- Yeast, ¼ Oz
- Whole grain flour, 4 tbsp.
- Salt, 1 tsp., and brown sugar, ¼ cup

- Egg, 1 large
- Butter, 2 tbsp.

For filling

- Sugar, 1/3 cup
- Cinnamon powder, 2 tbsp.
- Melted butter, 3 tbsp.

Preparation/Procedure

1. Make the dough by combining all-purpose flour, whole grain flour, sugar, salt, egg, and yeast mixed in water. Kneel to make it smooth for 6-8 minutes. let it set.
2. Spread the dough, add butter, and sprinkle sugar and cinnamon on it. Make rolls.
3. Transfer the rolls to the slow cooker
4. Let it rise in the slow cooker for 3-4 hours at a low temperature.
5. Serve with icing of your choice.

Storage

Cover the container with a lid and store it in the refrigerator.

Reheating

Reheat in a microwave for 2 minutes.

Nutritional facts/values (per serving)

Calories: 240 | Fat: 7g | Carbohydrates: 42g | Protein: 4g | Sodium: 254mg | Potassium: 69mg | Sugar: 20g

4.8 Bacon wrapped potato

8 Servings | Preparation time: 15 mins | Cook time: 420 mins

Ingredients/Food list

- Baby potatoes, 2 cups
- Bacon of your choice, 1 cup
- Chopped onions, 2
- Grated parmesan cheese, 4 tbsp.
- Shredded cheddar cheese, 1-½ cup
- Eggs, 6
- Milk, ½ cup
- All-purpose flour, 2 tbsp.
- Salt and pepper according to your taste.

Preparation/Procedure

1. Combine milk, eggs, flour, and seasonings in a bowl.
2. Make layers of ingredients in the slow cooker: potatoes, bacon, onions, and both kinds of cheese.
3. Repeat these layers and end with cheddar cheese.
4. Pour the egg mixture on top of the layers.
5. Let it cook slowly in the slow cooker for 7 hours at a low temperature.
6. Check it after 5 hours as well it may be done at that time too according to some small cookers.
7. Serve with your favorite sauce.

Storage

Cover the container with a lid and store it in the refrigerator.

Reheating

Reheat in a microwave for 2 minutes.

Nutritional facts/values (per serving)

Calories: 518 | Fat: 35g | Carbohydrates: 24g | Protein: 30g | Sodium: 1100mg | Calcium: 436mg | Sugar: 2g

4.9 Multi-grain porridge

6 Servings | Preparation time: 15 mins | Cook time: 360 mins

Ingredients/Food list

- Water, 5 cups
- Coarse oats, 3 tbsp.
- Cracked wheat, 3 tbsp.
- Brown rice, 3 tbsp.
- Barley, 2 tbsp.
- Cornmeal yellow, 2 tbsp.
- Millet brown rice, 2 tbsp.
- Mixed dry fruits, 1 cup
- Salt, ¼ tsp.
- Cinnamon powder, 1 tsp.
- Vanilla, 1 tsp.
- Fat-free milk

Preparation/Procedure

1. Add water, dry fruit, all grains (pre-toasted), vanilla, salt, and cinnamon to the slow cooker.
2. Cook for 7 hours until it absorbs all the liquid and becomes soft after cooking.
3. After cooking stir it well, if it's too thick add a little amount of boiling water and stir again.
4. Serve with milk, dry fruits, and cinnamon powder sprinkled.

Storage

Cover the container with a lid and store it in the refrigerator.

Reheating

It is not necessary, just keep it at room temperature for a few minutes.

Nutritional facts/values (per serving)

Calories: 322 | Fat: 11g | Carbohydrates: 55g | Protein: 10g | Sodium: 175mg | Potassium: 502mg | Sugar: 26g

4.10 Crunchy granola

8 Servings | Preparation time: 22 mins | Cook time: 210 mins

Ingredients/Food list

- Whole dates, 2 tbsp.
- Raisins, 2 tbsp.
- Flaxseeds, 1 tbsp.
- Sunflower kernels, ¼ cup

- Regular oats, 2-½ cup
- Peanut butter, 2 tbsp.
- Apple sauce, ¼ cup and honey, ¼ cup
- Cinnamon powder, 1 tsp.
- Canola oil, 2 tbsp.

Preparation/Procedure
1. Spray the slow cooker with cooking spray lightly.
2. Mix applesauce, honey, peanut butter, oil, and cinnamon in a small bowl.
3. Add oats, flaxseeds, sunflower kernels, and the mixture to the small cooker. Combine them properly.
4. Cook for 2-1/2 hours until fully toasted.
5. After cooking stir it well, if it's too thick add a little amount of boiling water and stir again.
6. Coat the cooked granola with dates and raisins.

Storage
Cover the container with a lid and store it at room temperature for 1 week or in the freezer for 2 months.
Reheating
It is not necessary, just keep it at room temperature.
Nutritional facts/values (per serving)
Calories: 234 | Fat: 10g | Carbohydrates: 35g | Protein: 5g | Sodium: 35mg | Potassium: 136mg | Sugar: 15g

4.11 Slow cooker carrot cake

6 Servings | Preparation time: 10 mins | Cook time: 480 mins
Ingredients/Food list
- Carrots shredded, 1 cup
- Steel-cut oats, 1-½ cups
- Water, 6 cups
- Salt, ¼ tsp.
- Cinnamon powder, 2 tsp.
- Nutmeg powder, ½ tsp.
- Mixed dry fruits, 1 cup (Optional)

Preparation/Procedure
1. Spray the slow cooker with cooking spray.
2. Mix water, oats, carrots, and salt.
3. Cook for 8 hours at a low temperature until it absorbs all the liquid and becomes soft after cooking.
4. Serve with toppings (dry fruits, nutmeg, and cinnamon powder sprinkled).

Storage
Cover the container with a lid and store it in the refrigerator for 4-5 days or freeze it in the freezer for up to 6 months.
Reheating
Reheat in the microwave
If using a stove, add water and milk to preserve consistency.

Nutritional facts/values (per serving)

Calories: 170 | Fat: 6g | Carbohydrates: 30g | Protein: 7g | Sodium: 120mg | Potassium: 70mg | Sugar: 1g

4.12 Vegetable omelet

8 Servings | Preparation time: 10 mins | Cook time: 210 mins

Ingredients/Food list

- Milk, ½ cup
- Grated cheese, ¼ cup
- Eggs, 8
- Salt, according to your taste
- Black pepper powder, garlic powder, chili powder, (according to your taste)
- Red bell pepper, 1 small
- Onion and garlic, (quantity of your choice)

Preparation/Procedure

1. Spray the slow cooker with cooking spray.
2. Mix eggs, cheese, milk, salt, chili powder, pepper powder, and garlic powder in a bowl.
3. Whisk and beat the mixture well.
4. Add bell pepper, onion, and garlic to the slow cooker. Spread egg mixture on them
5. Cook for 3.5 hours at a low temperature until becomes soft after cooking.
6. Garnish with cheese, onions, or tomatoes.
7. Serve with bread of your choice.

Storage

Cover the container with a lid and store it in the refrigerator.

Reheating

Reheat in the microwave

Nutritional facts/values (per serving)

Calories: 160 | Fat: 11g | Carbohydrates: 6g | Protein: 7g | Sodium: 220mg | Potassium: 180mg | Sugar: 2g

4.13 Breakfast soup with bread

6 Servings | Preparation time: 10 mins | Cook time: 480 mins

Ingredients/Food list

- Sausage links, 2 cups
- Cooked bacon, ½ cup
- Potatoes diced, 2 cups
- Eggs, 4
- Tomatoes diced, 1 cup
- Chicken broth, 4 cups
- Garlic, 2 cloves
- Hollandaise sauce, 1 packet

Preparation/Procedure

1. Add the potatoes, undrained tomatoes, and sausage to the slow cooker.

2. Add the broth, garlic, and hollandaise sauce to a mixing bowl.
3. Stir everything together until it is well-combined and smooth. Fill the slow cooker with the mixture.
4. Cook for 8 hours at a low temperature.
5. Add scrambled eggs and bacon to each bowl after ladling the soup into them.
6. Serve with hearty, crusty bread such as fresh toast, morning biscuits, or other.

Storage

Cover the container with a lid and store it in the refrigerator for 2-3 days or freeze it in the freezer for up to 6 months.

Reheating

Reheat in the microwave.

If using a stove, reheat on low flame.

Nutritional facts/values (per serving)

Calories: 570 | Fat: 6g | Carbohydrates: 15g | Protein: 38g | Sodium: 1507mg | Potassium: 996mg | Sugar: 3g

4.14 Fancy French toast

6 Servings | Preparation time: 20 mins | Cook time: 420 mins

Ingredients/Food list

- Brioche bread, (1–2-inch pieces) 22 Oz.
- Milk, 3 cups
- Cinnamon and Vanilla extract, 2 tsp.
- Powered nutmeg, Sea salt, ¼ tsp.
- Eggs, 8
- Garlic, 2 cloves
- Brown sugar, ½ cup
- Butter, ½ cup

Preparation/Procedure

1. Put the bread cubes in the oven for 15 minutes at 170F to dry.
2. Add the eggs, milk, vanilla, cinnamon, nutmeg, and salt to a bowl. Blend well by whisking.
3. Coat the bread pieces with this mixture. Place the bowl in the refrigerator with the cover on for at least two hours.
4. Combine the butter and brown sugar.
5. Transfer the bread pieces into the slow cooker and pour the butter mixture on top. Cook for 7 hours at a low temperature.
6. Add scrambled eggs and bacon to each bowl after ladling the soup into them.
7. Serve it with fresh strawberries, blueberries, maple syrup, and powdered sugar.

Storage

Cover the container with a lid and store it in the refrigerator.

Reheating

Reheat in the microwave.

Nutritional facts/values (per serving)

Calories: 480 | Fat: 26g | Carbohydrates: 48.7g | Protein: 14g | Sodium: 334mg | Potassium: 329mg | Sugar: 1.7g

5 BREADS

5.1 Slow cooker zucchini bread

10 Servings | Preparation time: 10 mins | Cook time: 300 mins

Ingredients/Food list

- Almond flour, 1 cup
- Coconut flour, ¼ cup
- Baking powder, 1-½ tsp.
- Eggs, 3
- Butter or coconut oil, 1/3 cup
- Cinnamon powder, 2 tsp.
- Vanilla, 2 tsp.
- Shredded Zucchini, 2cups
- Sugar substitute, 1 cup

Preparation/Procedure

1. Mix thoroughly with coconut flour, almond flour, cinnamon, baking soda, and salt. Blend the oil, eggs, vanilla, and sugar in a large bowl. To the wet mixture, add the dry ingredients.
2. Mix in the chopped nuts and the shredded zucchini.
3. Fill the prepared pan with the batter. Place the pan in the slow cooker using over a rack.
4. Cook for 5 hours at a low temperature.
5. Serve cold for the best taste.

Storage

Cover the container with a lid and store it in the refrigerator.

Reheating

No need to reheat.

Nutritional facts/values (per serving)

Calories: 178 | Fat: 16g | Carbohydrates: 13g | Protein: 5g | Sodium: 255mg | Potassium: 100mg | Sugar: 8g

5.2 Coconut bread

12 Servings | Preparation time: 10 mins | Cook time: 290 mins

Ingredients/Food list

- Cornmeal (yellow), 2 cups
- All-purpose flour, 2 cups
- Shredded coconut, 1-½ cups
- Baking powder, 1-½ tsp.
- Milk, 2 cups
- Eggs, 2
- Butter or coconut oil, ½ cup
- Sugar substitute, ½ cup

Preparation/Procedure

1. Take cornmeal, all-purpose flour, coconut, baking soda, sugar, and salt, and mix thoroughly in a bowl. Blend the oil, eggs, milk, and in another large bowl.
2. To the wet mixture, add the dry ingredients.
3. Fill the prepared pan with the batter. Place the pan in the slow cooker using over a rack.
4. Cook for 5 hours at a low temperature.
5. Cut into 12 pieces and serve.

Storage

Cover the container with a lid and store it in the refrigerator.

Reheating

No need to reheat.

Nutritional facts/values (per serving)

Calories: 587 | Fat: 23 g | Carbohydrates: 80g | Protein: 11g | Sodium: 467mg | Potassium: 112mg | Sugar: 14g

5.3 Banana-Nutella bread

8 Servings | Preparation time: 30 mins | Cook time: 60 mins

Ingredients/Food list

- All-purpose flour, 2 cups
- Mashed banana, 3 medium
- Nutella, ¾ cup
- Baking powder, ¾ tsp.
- Milk, 1/3 cup
- Eggs, 2
- Butter, ¼ cup
- Granulated sugar, 1 cup
- Vanilla extract, 1 tsp.
- Salt, ½ tsp.

Preparation/Procedure

1. Take cornmeal, all-purpose flour, baking soda, and salt, and mix thoroughly in a bowl. Cream the sugar and butter in a separate bowl using a hand mixer, then add eggs one by one and mix.
2. Add milk, mashed bananas, and vanilla until fully combined.
3. To the wet mixture, add the dry ingredients slowly.
4. Microwave Nutella for 30 seconds until melted and smooth.
5. Add Nutella to 1 cup of bread batter and mix.
6. Fill the prepared pan with both batter layers. Place the pan in the slow cooker using over a rack.
7. Cook for 1 hour at a high temperature.
8. Serve warm for better taste.

Storage

Cover the container with a lid and store it in the refrigerator.

Reheating

No need to reheat.

Nutritional facts/values (per serving)

Calories: 537 | Fat: 14 g | Carbohydrates: 96g | Protein: 9g | Sodium: 278mg | Potassium: 299mg | Sugar: 47g

5.4 Slow cooker garlic bread

6 Servings | Preparation time: 5 mins | Cook time: 180 mins

Ingredients/Food list

- All-purpose flour, 2 cups
- Shredded Cheddar cheese, ½ cup
- Butter, ½ cup
- Garlic powder, ¼ tsp.
- Milk, 2/3 cup

Preparation/Procedure

1. Take all-purpose flour, and cheddar cheese, and mix thoroughly in a bowl. Mix with milk until fully combined.
2. Fill the prepared pan with batter. Place the pan in the slow cooker using over a rack.
3. Cook for 3 hours or until the center is fully cooked at a low temperature.
4. Melt the butter on the stove and add garlic powder to it. Brush the butter on the bread when it's cooked.
5. Serve warm for better taste.

Storage

Cover the container with a lid and store it in the refrigerator.

Reheating

No need to reheat.

Nutritional facts/values (per serving)

Calories: 533 | Fat: 14 g | Carbohydrates: 57g | Protein: 12g | Sodium: 278mg | Potassium: 885mg | Sugar: 5g

6 SOUPS AND STEWS

6.1 Creamy Potato Cheese Soup in the Slow Cooker

18 Servings | Preparation time: 30 mins | Cook time: 5 hours

Ingredients/Food list

- Butter, ¼ cup
- All-purpose flour, ¼ cup
- Minced white onion, ½ cup
- Water, 2 cups
- Chopped big carrots, 2
- Celery stalks, chopped, 4
- Chopped, dry garlic, 1 tsp.
- Pepper and salt as desired
- Milk, 1 cup
- The base for chicken soup is 2 tbsp.
- Hot water, 1 cup
- Diced and peeled russet, potatoes, 5 pounds
- Bay leaf, 1
- Cheddar cheese, 1 cup shredded
- Crumbled crisp fried bacon, 6 pieces

Preparation/Procedure

1. In a saucepan set over medium heat, melt the butter. The butter-cooked onion should be transparent. Gradually add the carrots, celery, garlic, salt, and pepper along with 2 cups of water. After fully heating, add milk and stir. Pour 1 cup of hot water with the chicken foundation already dissolved in it into the vegetable mixture.
2. Place the potatoes in the slow cooker, then add the hot vegetable mixture. Add a bay leaf to the saucepan.
3. Cook with a cover for either 5 hours on High or 8 hours on Low.
4. Delete the bay leaf. About 4 cups of the soup should be blended in a blender or food processor before being added to the slow cooker's contents. Cheese and bacon are added; stir until cheese is melted.

Storage

Cover the container with a lid and store it in the refrigerator.

Reheating

Reheat it in the pan or microwave it for 2 minutes.

Nutritional facts/values (per serving)

Calories: 169 | Fat: 5g | Carbohydrates: 27g | Protein: 5g | Sodium: 320mg | Potassium: 452mg | Sugar: 2g

6.2 Stew with beef cooked slowly

6 Servings | Preparation time: 20 mins | Cook time: 4hours 20 mins

Ingredients/Food list

- Beef stew meat, 2 pounds of 1-inch-long chunks

- All-purpose flour, 1/4 cup
- Salt and black pepper, ½ tsp. of each
- Beef broth, 12 ounces
- Medium potatoes, diced 3
- Medium carrots, sliced 3
- Medium onion, diced 1
- The chopped stalk of celery, 1
- Worcestershire sauce, 1 tsp.
- Paprika, ground 1 tsp.
- Minced garlic clove, 1
- Bay leaf, 1 inch-long

Preparation/Procedure

1. Add the meat to the slow cooker.
2. In a small bowl, stir together the flour, salt, and pepper. Stir the meat after pouring the sauce over it.
3. Stir in the beef broth, along with the carrots, potatoes, onion, celery, Worcestershire sauce, paprika, garlic, and bay leaf.
4. On Low for 8 to 12 hours or on High for 4 to 6 hours, cover and cook the meat until it can be sliced with a spoon.

Storage

Put the beef stew in a small, airtight container once it has cooled. For up to three days, keep in the refrigerator.

Reheating

Use the microwave or the stove to reheat.

Nutritional facts/values (per serving)

Calories: 576 | Fat: 30g | Carbohydrates: 30g | Protein: 44g | Sodium: 542mg | Potassium: 1187mg | Sugar: 4g

6.3 Beef-barley soup with vegetables

10 Servings | Preparation time: 20 mins | Cook time: 4hours 15 mins

Ingredients/Food list

- Chuck roast of beef, 1 (3-pound)
- Barley, ½ cup
- Oil, 2 tbsp.
- Bay leaf, 1
- Chopped carrots, 3
- Chopped celery stalks, 3
- Chopped onion, 1
- Mixed veggies, 16 ounces
- Water, 4 cups
- Chopped stewed tomatoes, 28 ounces
- Beef bouillon cube cubes, 4
- Crushed black pepper,1/4 tsp. or more to taste

- White sugar, 1 tbsp.

Preparation/Procedure

1. Chuck roast should be put in a slow cooker. 4 to 5 hours on high, or until meat is tender. Barley and a bay leaf should be added in the final hour of cooking.
2. Slice the removed meat into bite-sized pieces. Remove the bay leaf. Set aside the steak, broth, and barley.
3. In a large stockpot, heat the oil over medium-high heat. Cook the frOzen mixed veggies, carrots, celery, and onion for 5 to 7 minutes, or until they are soft. Add the beef-barley broth combination together with the water, stewed tomatoes, beef bouillon cubes, sugar, and 1/4 teaspoon of pepper. Bring to a boil, lower the heat, and simmer for ten to twenty minutes.
4. Before serving, season with salt and pepper.

Storage

Cover the container with a lid and store it in the refrigerator.

Reheating

Reheat it in the pan or microwave it for 2 minutes.

Nutritional facts/values (per serving)

Calories: 321 | Fat: 17g | Carbohydrates: 22g | Protein: 20g | Sodium: 606mg | Potassium: 553mg | Sugar: 6g

6.4 Oxtail Stew in a Slow Cooker

12 Servings | Preparation time: 20 mins | Cook time: 8hours 10 mins

Ingredients/Food list

- Vegetable oil, 1 tbsp.
- Cut-up beef oxtail, 3 pounds
- Chunked, peeled russet potatoes, 1 ½ pound of
- Carrots, peeled and chopped into substantial pieces, 4
- Celery stalks, chopped into big pieces, 3
- Tomato sauce, One (15 ounces), chopped onion, 1
- Beef broth, 1 cup
- Dry red wine, ½ Cup
- Freshly chopped parsley, 2 tsp.
- Worcestershire sauce, 1 serving
- Dried thyme, 1 tbsp.
- Smoked paprika, ½ tsp.
- Sliced mushrooms 8 ounces
- FrOzen peas, 1 cup
- Freshly ground black pepper, 1 pinch, and sprinkle salt as per taste

Preparation/Procedure

1. In a large skillet, heat the oil over medium-high heat. Oxtail is grilled for 4 minutes. About 4 minutes after flipping, continue frying until all sides are browned. Oxtail should be placed in a slow cooker.
2. The following ingredients should be added: paprika, thyme, Worcestershire sauce, parsley, , red wine, beef broth, tomato sauce, onion, celery, potatoes, and carrots.

3. on low for seven hours. Add peas and mushrooms to the dish. Cook for a another hour.

4. Season with salt and pepper after ladling into bowls.

Storage

Cover the container with a lid and store it in the refrigerator.

Reheating

Reheat it in the pan or microwave it for 2 minutes.

Nutritional facts/values (per serving)

Calories: 241 | Fat: 9g | Carbohydrates: 18g | Protein: 21g | Sodium: 428mg | Potassium: 687mg | Sugar: 5g

6.5 Lamb stew cooked slowly

4 Servings | Preparation time: 15 mins | Cook time: 7hours 25 mins

Ingredients/Food list

- Olive oil, 1 tbsp.
- Cubed stew meat from lamb, 1 pound
- Huge onion, cut into petals, 1
- Big cubed red potatoes, 1
- Fresh button mushrooms, 4
- Big carrots 2, celery stalks 2, and large carrots cut 2
- Beef stock, 2 cups
- Tomato paste 6 ounces
- Beer, ½ cup
- Worcestershire sauce, 3 tsp.
- Substantial sprig of fresh rosemary, 1
- Salt, and pepper as desired
- Frozen peas in 1 ½ cups

Preparation/Procedure

1. In a large skillet over medium heat, heat the oil. Add the lamb and onions; heat and stir for about 5 minutes, or until the meat has browned and the onions have begun to soften. Slow cooker should be filled with lamb mixture.

2. Mushrooms, potatoes, carrots, and celery should be added. Add rosemary, Worcestershire sauce, tomato paste, beer, salt, and pepper; then stir in the beef broth.

3. 7 hours on high for cooking. For a further 15 minutes, add the peas. Add salt and pepper to taste.

Storage

Cover the container with a lid and store it in the refrigerator.

Reheating

Reheat it in the pan or microwave it for 2 minutes.

Nutritional facts/values (per serving)

Calories: 438 | Fat: 17g | Carbohydrates: 46g | Protein: 27g | Sodium: 1053mg | Potassium: 1697mg | Sugar: 15g

6.6   Chicken Pot Pie Stew in the Slow Cooker

16 Servings | Preparation time: 20 mins | Cook time: 6hours

Ingredients/Food list

- Big skinless, boneless chicken breast halves, 4 pieces
- Medium red potatoes, quartered, 10
- Condensed cream of chicken soup 26 ounces
- Baby carrots 8 ounces
- Celery, chopped, 1 cup
- Chicken bouillon cubes, 6
- Black pepper, ground, 1 tbsp.
- Salt and garlic, 2 tbsp.
- Salt for celery, 1 tsp.
- Mixed veggies 16-ounce

Preparation/Procedure

1. In a slow cooker, combine the following ingredients: potatoes, chicken, condensed soup, carrots, celery, pepper, bouillon, garlic salt, and celery salt. Cover and cook on High for 5 hours.
2. After adding frOzen mixed veggies, heat on high for an additional hour.

Storage

Cover the container with a lid and store it in the refrigerator.

Reheating

Reheat it in the pan or microwave it for 2 minutes.

Nutritional facts/values (per serving)

Calories: 263 | Fat: 7g | Carbohydrates: 34g | Protein: 17g | Sodium: 1416mg | Potassium: 849mg | Sugar: 3g

6.7   Ham and lentil soup cooked slowly

6 Servings | Preparation time: 20 mins | Cook time: 11hours

Ingredients/Food list

- Dry lentils, 1 cup
- Celery and carrots, each cup diced
- Onion, chopped, 1 cup
- Minced garlic cloves, 2
- Cooked ham diced 1 ½ cup
- Dried basil, ½ tsp.
- Dry thyme, ¼ tsp.
- Dried oregano, ½ tsp.
- Black pepper, 1/4 tsp., bay leaf, 1
- Tomato sauce, 8tbsp.
- Water 1 cup
- Chicken broth, 32 ounces

Preparation/Procedure

1. Lentils, celery, carrots, onion, garlic, and ham should all be combined in a slow cooker with a capacity of at least 3 1/2 quarts. Add pepper, bay leaf, oregano, basil, and thyme to season.
2. Add the tomato sauce, water, and chicken broth while stirring. For 11 hours on Low, cook covered. Before serving, throw away the bay leaf.

Storage
Cover the container with a lid and store it in the refrigerator.

Reheating
Reheat it in the pan or microwave it for 2 minutes.

Nutritional facts/values (per serving)
Calories: 222 | Fat: 6g | Carbohydrates:26 g | Protein: 15g | Sodium: 1170mg | Potassium: 594mg | Sugar: 4g

6.8 Potato-Bacon Soup in the Slow Cooker

10 Servings | Preparation time: 15 mins | Cook time: 6hours 15 mins

Ingredients/Food list

- Bacon, 9 pieces
- Peeled and cubed potatoes, 7
- Coarsely diced onion, 1
- Powdered garlic, 1tsp.
- Vegetable broth, 3 cups
- Regular flour, 2 tbsp.
- Cheddar-Monterey Jack cheese combination, 3 1/4 cups,
- Split fresh chives, cut into a teaspoon-size piece, or to taste (Optional)

Preparation/Procedure

1. In a large pan, add the bacon, and cook for about 10 minutes, flipping the bacon regularly, until it is uniformly browned. Slices of bacon should be dried off using paper towels; save the pan drippings. 6 slices of bacon should be crumbled; save 3 for garnish.
2. Bacon drippings are heated over medium-high heat. In the heated drippings, cook the onion for approximately 5 minutes, or until tender.
3. Add potatoes, bacon that has been crumbled, onions, and garlic powder to a slow cooker. Over the top, pour the broth. Potatoes should be cooked on Low for around 6 hours.
4. Flour and half-and-half are combined in a bowl. Add the potatoes to the slow cooker and mash some of them with a whisk. Add 3 cups of a Cheddar-Monterey Jack cheese mixture by stirring. Mix until all of the cheese is melted and combined.
5. Crumble any leftover bacon.
6. Before serving, sprinkle the remaining cheese, bacon bits, and chives on top.

Storage
Cover the container with a lid and store it in the refrigerator.

Reheating
Reheat it in the pan or microwave it for 2 minutes.

Nutritional facts/values (per serving)
Calories: 380 | Fat: 20g | Carbohydrates: 35g | Protein: 16g | Sodium: 581mg | Potassium: 777mg | Sugar: 3g

6.9 Remaining Turkey Soup (Slow Cooker)

8 Servings | Preparation time: 20 mins | Cook time: 10 hours

Ingredients/Food list

- Turkey carcass with flesh and skin
- Removed, 1
- Chicken broth, 2 quarts of
- Onion, ¼
- Lengthwise-cut carrots, 2
- Lengthwise-cut celery stalks, 3
- Bay leaf, 2
- Carrots, chopped, 1 cup
- Chopped onion, ¼ cup
- Chopped celery, 1/3 cup
- Penne pasta, 2 cups
- Cooked turkey, chopped 3 cups
- Condensed cream of mushroom soup (10.75 ounces) can (optional)

Preparation/Procedure

1. In a slow cooker, combine the turkey carcass, chicken stock, onion quarters, carrot halves, celery halves, and bay leaves.
2. 4 hours on high for cooking. The broth should be carefully strained, sediments discarded, and then transferred to a bowl. Clean the cooker.
3. Add chopped carrots, celery, and onion to the slow cooker after adding the liquid once more.
4. 3 hours on low heat. Cook the penne pasta in the slow cooker for an additional 2 1/2 hours.
5. Cook for a further 30 minutes after adding turkey meat and cream of mushroom soup to the soup.

Storage

Cover the container with a lid and store it in the refrigerator.

Reheating

Reheat it in the pan or microwave it for 2 minutes.

Nutritional facts/values (per serving)

Calories: 1877 | Fat: 141g | Carbohydrates: 55g | Protein: 93g | Sodium: 1542mg | Potassium: 1281mg | Sugar: 8g

6.10 Mediterranean lentil stew prepared slowly

10 Servings | Preparation time: 20 mins | Cook time: 3hours 10 mins

Ingredients/Food list

- Water, 5 glasses
- Vegetable bouillon cubes, 2 ½ cubes, or more to taste
- Lentils, dry 2 cups
- Tiny carrots, 5 chopped after being peeled
- Medium potatoes, 2 diced after being peeled
- Cumin powder, 3 tbsp., or to taste
- Coriander, ground 1 tsp.

- Olive oil, 1 tbsp.
- Chopped tiny onion, 1
- Minced garlic cloves, 4
- Tomato paste, 1/2 (6 ounces) or as desired, sea salt, ½ tsp. or as desired
- Freshly ground black pepper, as desired, ½ tsp.
- Shredded fresh spinach, 8 ounces

Preparation/Procedure
1. In a slow cooker on High, heat water and veggie bouillon until the bouillon is dissolved. Add the potatoes, carrots, and lentils.
2. Over medium heat, warm a medium saucepan. Cook and whisk the cumin and coriander for 20 seconds, or until aromatic. Add the onion after the oil. Cook for 2 to 3 minutes, stirring periodically. Stir in the garlic for 30 seconds. Transfer to the slow cooker after removing from the heat. Stir. Add salt, pepper, and tomato paste. Add spinach and stir.
3. Cook on High, stirring every 30 minutes, for 3 to 4 hours, or until the lentils are cooked and the stew has thickened.

Storage
Cover the container with a lid and store it in the refrigerator.
Reheating
Reheat it in the pan or microwave it for 2 minutes.
Nutritional facts/values (per serving)
Calories: 208 | Fat: 2g | Carbohydrates: 36g | Protein: 12g | Sodium: 194mg | Potassium: 805mg | Sugar: 4g

6.11 Hickory bone soup

4 Servings | Preparation time: 30 mins | Cook time: 6hours
Ingredients/Food list
- Peeled and diced tomatoes with liquid, 1 (14.5 ounces)
- Chopped onion, 1
- Ham bone with some flesh, 1
- Kidney beans 15.25 ounce
- Green bell pepper, seeded, 1
- Diced potatoes, 3
- Water,4 glasses
- Chicken bouillon cubes, 6

Preparation/Procedure
1. In a 3 quart or larger slow cooker, combine the ham bone, onion, tomatoes, kidney beans, potatoes, and green pepper. Pour the dissolved bouillon cubes and water into the slow cooker.
2. Warm up under cover while cooking on high. Cook for a further 5 to 6 hours on Low heat.

Storage
Reheat it in the pan or microwave it for 2 minutes.
Reheating
It is not necessary, just keep it at room temperature for a few minutes.
Nutritional facts/values (per serving)

Calories: 266 | Fat: 1g | Carbohydrates: 53g | Protein: 11g | Sodium: 2136mg | Potassium: 920mg | Sugar: 6g

6.12 Mexican beef stew cooked slowly

6 Servings | Preparation time: 15 mins | Cook time: 7hours 15 mins

Ingredients/Food list

- Liner for a slow cooker, 1
- Beef stew meat, 1 pound of 1-inch-long chunks
- Regular flour, 2tbsp.
- Canola oil, 1 tbsp.
- Rinsed and drained black beans, 15 ounces
- Chop medium carrots after peeling them, 2
- Medium onion, 1 minced
- Garlic cloves, minced, 2
- Undrained diced tomatoes, 14.5 ounces
- Beef broth with reduced sodium, 14.5 ounces
- Chili powder, 1 1/2 tbsp.
- Cumin, 1 tsp.
- Salt, ½ tsp.
- Black pepper, ¼ tsp.
- Chopped avocado, and cilantro, ¼ cup each
- Crushed red pepper and 1 cup of frOzen whole-kernel corn (optional)

Preparation/Procedure

1. Use a slow cooker liner to line a 5- to 6-quart slow cooker. Beef should be floured.
2. In a large skillet, heat the oil over medium-high heat. Add the meat and heat and stir for 5 to 7 minutes, or until browned.
3. Beans, carrots, onion, and garlic should be added to the lined slow cooker. Add browned meat on top. Tomatoes, broth, cumin, chili powder, salt, and pepper should be added.
4. For 7 hours or until the meat is tender to the fork, cover and simmer on low.
5. Utilizing a rubber spatula, add the corn gradually. 10 more minutes under cover, or until cooked all the way through. Serve with avocado, cilantro, and/or crushed red pepper, as preferred.

Storage

Cover the container with a lid and store it in the refrigerator.

Reheating

Reheat it in the pan or microwave it for 2 minutes.

Nutritional facts/values (per serving)

Calories: 272 | Fat: 9g | Carbohydrates: 27g | Protein: 22g | Sodium: 647mg | Potassium: 731mg | Sugar: 5g

7   GRAINS AND BEANS

7.1   Beans and grains in a slow cooker

3 Servings | Preparation time: 6 hours | Cook time: 10 hours

Ingredients/Food list

PM

- Dried beans, 2 cups of any kind except kidney beans
- Water, 4 cups

Am

- Water in the morning, 2 cups
- Tomatoes or puree, 1 can (15.5 Oz.) Diced
- To make gluten-free, substitute quinoa or more millet for 1/4 cup of bulgur
- Millet ¼ cup
- Dry veggie bouillon, 1 tbsp. Flavored with nutritional yeast or chicken cube
- Cumin, 1 tbsp.
- Chilli spice blend, 1 tsp.
- Ancho or chipotle powder, ½ tsp.
- Smoked paprika salt, ½ tsp.

Preparation/Procedure

1. The night before, combine the beans and water in a slow cooker and cook on low for at least 7 to 8 hours.
2. In the morning, carefully drain and rinse the beans. Then add the freshwater, grains, tomatoes, and all spices except the salt to the slow cooker.
3. Cook on low heat for 7 to 10 hours.
4. Before serving, season with salt to taste.

Storage

Cover the container with a lid and store it in the refrigerator.

Reheating

Reheat it in the pan or microwave it for 2 minutes.

Nutritional facts/values (per serving)

Calories: 502 | Fat: 0.9g | Carbohydrates: 119g | Protein: 6g | Sodium: 1765mg | Potassium: 515mg | Sugar: 93g

7.2   Pinto Beans with Diced Ham in the slow cooker

4-6 Servings | Preparation time: 10 mins | Cook time: 7hours

Ingredients/Food list

- Rinsed and drained pinto beans, 2 cans (16 ounces each)
- 1 cup cooked diced ham, 1 can (14.5 ounces)
- Sauce with tomatoes, 1 can (8 ounces) (8 ounces)
- Medium finely chopped onion, 1
- Bell pepper, chopped ½ cup
- Celery, chopped ½ cup

- Carrot, chopped ½ cup
- Black pepper, ground ½ tsp.
- Chilli powder, ½ tsp.
- Cumin powder, ½ tsp.
- Oregano leaf, ¼ tsp.
- Garlic powder, 1 tbsp.
- Salt, or as desired ¼ tsp.

Preparation/Procedure
1. In the slow cooker, combine all of the listed ingredients and stir to combine.
2. Cook the beans in the slow cooker on low for 5 to 7 hours, or until the vegetables are tender.
3. Before serving, stir to combine.

Storage
Cover the container with a lid and store it in the refrigerator.
Reheating
Reheat it in the pan or microwave it for 2 minutes.
Nutritional facts/values (per serving)
Calories: 566 | Fat: 3g | Carbohydrates: 104g | Protein: 36g | Sodium: 200 mg | Potassium: 2981mg | Sugar: 22g

7.3 Red Beans and Rice with Andouille Sausage in the slow cooker

6-8 Servings | Preparation time: 20 mins | Cook time: 8hours
Ingredients/Food list
- Dried small red beans, also known as kidney beans, 1 pound
- Water, 1.5 quarts
- Celery (3 stalks, diced or sliced)
- Chopped onion, 1 large
- Minced garlic cloves, 2
- Bay leaves, 2
- Crushed red pepper flakes (or more as desired), ½ tsp.
- Vegetable oil, 1 tbsp.
- Diced spicy andouille sausage, 1 pound
- Green bell pepper, diced ½ cup
- Kosher salt, or to taste 2-3 tsp.
- Whole-grain rice, 2 cups
- Optional: freshly baked cornbread for serving

Preparation/Procedure
1. Collect all of the ingredients.
2. To rinse the dried beans, agitate them in a dish of cold water. Remove any beans that float.
3. Examine the beans in the colander for any small stones or misshapen beans.
4. Place the beans in the crockery insert of the slow cooker.
5. crushed red pepper flakes, bay leaves, , garlic, onion, celery and 1 1/2 quarts water should be added to the beans.

6. Cover the slow cooker and cook on low for 6.5 hours, or until the beans are cooked. Alternately, cook them on high for three and a half to five hours.
7. Heat the vegetable oil in a pan over medium heat. Cook the andouille sausage with constant stirring until it is beautifully browned.
8. Add the meat and bell pepper to the beans. Or, taste and season with two teaspoons of kosher salt.
9. Cover and cook for an additional hour over low heat.
10. Cook the rice according to the instructions on the package in a rice cooker or on the stovetop.
11. If preferred, serve with freshly made bread or cornbread.

Storage

Cover the container with a lid and store it in the refrigerator.

Reheating

Reheat it in the pan or microwave it for 2 minutes.

Nutritional facts/values (per serving)

Calories: 327 | Fat: 18g | Carbohydrates: 28g | Protein: 13g | Sodium: 962mg | Potassium: 603mg | Sugar: 2g

7.4 Slow cooker Hotdogs and beans

8 Servings | Preparation time: 10 mins | Cook time: 5hours 10 mins

Ingredients/Food list

- Pork and beans, 1 can (28 ounces)
- Great northern beans that have been rinsed and drained, 1 can (15 ounces
- Rinsed and drained black beans, 1 (15-ounce) can
- Chopped green or red bell pepper, 1
- Minced onion, ½ cup
- Light brown sugar, 1/3 cup
- Barbecue sauce, 1/3 cup
- Ketchup, 1/4 cup
- Molasses, 2 tbsp. or maple syrup
- Chilli powder, 10 grams
- Salt, 1 tsp.
- Cumin powder, 1/8 tsp.
- Freshly ground black pepper, ½ teaspoon

Preparation/Procedure

1. Assemble the components.
2. Cut hot dogs into lengths of 1 to 2 inches. Reserve.
3. All ingredients should be combined in a 4- to 6-quart slow cooker.
4. For 5 to 6 hours, cook on low with a cover.
5. After that, serve and take pleasure

Storage

Cover the container with a lid and store it in the refrigerator.

Reheating

Reheat it in the pan or microwave it for 2 minutes.

Nutritional facts/values (per serving) Calories: 463 | Fat: 19g | Carbohydrates: 59g | Protein: 19g | Sodium: 1700mg | Potassium: 900mg | Sugar: 18g

7.5 Beans Slow-Cooked with 5 Ingredients with Bacon

6 Servings | Preparation time: 15mins | Cook time: 5hours

Ingredients/Food list

- Sliced into 1/2-inch chunks, 6 to 8 slices of bacon.
- Brown sugar packed 14 cups
- Mustard powder, 1 ½ tsp.
- Ketchup, 1/2 cup (or chili sauce)
- Baked beans, 3 cans each 16 ounces

Preparation/Procedure

1. Assemble the ingredients
2. Place a pan over medium heat and add the chopped bacon. Cook the bacon for 8 to 10 minutes, tossing and rotating it periodically until it is crisp and browned.
3. bacon is fried for baked beans.
4. To drain, remove the bacon and place it on paper towels.
5. Draining bacon on paper towels
6. Stir together the ketchup or chili sauce, mustard powder, and brown sugar in a bowl. Place the bacon in the slow cooker after adding the beans and stirring. Mix the beans with the sauce mixture thoroughly.
7. Beans in the slow cooker, baked.
8. Cook covered for 4 to 5 hours on low or around 2 hours on high. Enjoy after serving.

Storage

Cover the container with a lid and store it in the refrigerator.

Reheating

Reheat it in the pan or microwave it for 2 minutes.

Nutritional facts/values (per serving)

Calories: 241 | Fat: 6g | Carbohydrates: 40g | Protein: 11g | Sodium: 877mg | Potassium: 429mg | Sugar: 22g

7.6 Baked beans in a slow cooker

8 Servings | Preparation time: 10 mins | Cook time: 14 hours

Ingredients/Food list

- Great northern beans in dry form, 1 pound
- Chopped salt pork, 4 ounces in 8 cups of water
- Onion, chopped 1 cup
- Molasses, 1/2 cup
- Brown sugar in bags 1/3 cup
- Dried mustard 1 tbsp.
- Black pepper, ground 1/8 tsp.

Preparation/Procedure

1. Put the Great Northern Beans and water in a big pot the night before. Boiling for 1 1/2 hours is followed by cooking. Put the beans and their liquid in a bowl, cover it and put it in the fridge for the night.
2. Drain out the liquid in the morning, saving 1 cup. Fill the slow cooker's crock with the beans and the liquid that was set aside. Add the mustard, pepper, molasses, brown sugar, onion, salt, and pork. Cook on Low for 12 to 14 hours with the cover on. Before serving, stir.

Storage

Cover the container with a lid and store it in the refrigerator.

Reheating

Reheat it in the pan or microwave it for 2 minutes.

Nutritional facts/values (per serving)

Calories: 364 | Fat: 12g | Carbohydrates: 54g | Protein: 12g | Sodium: 223mg | Potassium: 864mg | Sugar: 21g

7.7 Savoury grains cooked slowly

6 Servings | Preparation time: 25 mins | Cook time: 6 hour 30 mins

Ingredients/Food list

- Long-grain brown rice, uncooked 1 cup
- Uncooked wild rice, ½ cup
- Green lentils, raw ½ cup
- Sliced up fresh mushrooms 3 cups (8 Oz)
- Medium carrots, 2 cut coarsely (1 cup)
- Chopped medium green onions, 12 (about 3/4 cup)
- Broth made with chicken or roasted vegetables (4 cups) in one container (32 Oz.)
- Water, 1 cup
- Soy sauce with less sodium, 2 tbsp. If preferred, 2 tablespoons of dry sherry
- Melted butter 2 tbsp. Or margarine
- Thyme leaves, dried ½ tsp.
- Salt with garlic, ½ tsp.
- Toasted, chopped walnuts ¼ cup
- Parsley, chopped finely 1/3 cup

Preparation/Procedure

1. Combine all ingredients in a 3- to a 4-quart slow cooker, leaving out the parsley and walnuts.
2. Cook on Low heat for 6 to 7 hours and 30 minutes with a cover on.
3. Before serving, stir. Combine with walnuts and parsley.

Storage

Cover the container with a lid and store it in the refrigerator.

Reheating

Reheat it in the pan or microwave it for 2 minutes.

Nutritional facts/values (per serving)

Calories: 330 | Fat: 9g | Carbohydrates: 51g | Protein: 12g | Sodium: 980mg | Potassium: 550mg | Sugar: 5g

7.8 Wheat Cereal is Prepared Slowly

4-6 Servings | Preparation time: 10 mins | Cook time: 10 hour

Ingredients/Food list

- Either soft white or firm red wheat berries (rinsed), 2 cups
- Water in 4 glasses
- Fruit, chopped (optional)
- Raisins, 8
- Vanilla extract, 1/2 tsp.
- Brown sugar, 2 tbsp. (add more for a sweeter taste)
- Cinnamon, 1 tsp.
- Allspice, 1/2 tsp.
- Cloves, ground, 12 tsp.
- Sliced almonds in a cup (optional)

Preparation/Procedure

1. All ingredients should be combined and cooked overnight on low heat in a slow cooker. Hard red berries take longer to cook than delicate white berries.
2. For optimal results with hard red berries, give it at least 10 hours. If preferred, swap sugar for stevia extract. Once cooked, garnish with your preferred toppings and devour!

Storage

Cover the container with a lid and store it in the refrigerator.

Reheating

Reheat it in the pan or microwave it for 2 minutes.

Nutritional facts/values (per serving)

Calories: 1526 | Fat: 7.97g | Carbohydrates: 327.39g | Protein: 60.4g | Sodium: 43mg | Potassium: 1554mg | Sugar: 62.05g

7.9 Slow-Cooker Chili with 3 Beans

8 Servings | Preparation time: 10 mins | Cook time: 10hours 5 mins

Ingredients/Food list

- Rinsed and drained black beans, 15 ounces
- Washed and drained garbanzo beans, 15 ounces
- rinsed and drained kidney beans, 15.5 ounces
- Dried lentils, 1 cup sorted and rinsed (8 ounces).
- Big crumbled vegetarian or chicken bouillon cube, 1
- Chilli seasoning mix in one envelope, 1.25 ounces
- Tomato sauce, 15 ounces
- Undrained diced tomatoes, 10 ounces, and water, 3 cups

Preparation/Procedure

1. In a 3- to the 4-quart slow cooker, combine all the ingredients except the tomatoes and tomato sauce.
2. Cook for 8 to 10 hours with a cover over a low heat setting.

3. Add tomatoes and tomato sauce and stir. Turn up the heat setting. 5 minutes under cover, or until heated all the way through.

Storage
Cover the container with a lid and store it in the refrigerator.

Reheating
Reheat it in the pan or microwave it for 2 minutes.

Nutritional facts/values (per serving)
Calories: 575 | Fat: 18.05g | Carbohydrates: 83.27g | Protein: 25.93g | Sodium: 2712mg | Potassium: 3911mg | Sugar: 7.67g

7.10 Recipe for Pearled Grain Cooked Slowly

1 Servings | Preparation time: 5 mins | Cook time: 4hours

Ingredients/Food list
Pearled sorghum grain, 1 cup

Stock or water, 3 cups

Preparation/Procedure
1. Pearled grain sorghum should be rinsed and drained.
2. Sorghum and liquid should be added to a slow cooker. For four hours, set the slow cooker to high. If necessary, stir.
3. Drain the sorghum into a small mesh strainer when the slow cooker is finished cooking. After rinsing, fluff the sorghum using a fork. Add the grain or other components to your preferred recipe.

Storage
Cover the container with a lid and store it in the refrigerator.

Reheating
Reheat it in the pan or microwave it for 2 minutes.

Nutritional facts/values (per serving)
Calories: 1202 | Fat: 107.03g | Carbohydrates: 49.65g | Protein: 17.13g | Sodium: 1994mg | Potassium: 470mg | Sugar: 11.73g

7.11 Slow-cooker Beans Made at Home

12 Servings | Preparation time: 20 mins | Cook time: 8hours

Ingredients/Food list
- Dry navy beans, 3 cups cooked for an hour or overnight.
- Thickly sliced bacon slices, 6 divided into 1-inch-long chunks
- Chopped onion, 1 big
- Ketchup, 1 1/2 cups
- Water 1 ½ cups
- Molasses, ¼ cup and brown sugar, 1 cup
- Dried mustard, 1/9 cup
- Salt, 1tsp.

Preparation/Procedure
1. Beans should be drained of their soaking liquid and put in a slow cooker.

2. Beans should be thoroughly mixed with the bacon, onion, ketchup, water, brown sugar, molasses, mustard, and salt.

3. Cook on Low for 8 to 10 hours with the cover on, stirring if necessary.

Storage

Cover the container with a lid and store it in the refrigerator.

Reheating

Reheat it in the pan or microwave it for 2 minutes.

Nutritional facts/values (per serving)

Calories: 296 | Fat: 3g | Carbohydrates: 57g | Protein: 12g | Sodium: 1312mg | Potassium: 741mg | Sugar: 23g

7.12 Pinto beans cooked slowly

8 Servings | Preparation time: 15 mins | Cook time: 5hours 15 mins

Ingredients/Food list

- Dried pinto beans, 1 pound, soaking overnight
- Cubed 1 pound of Black Forest ham,
- Medium onion, 1
- Medium green bell pepper, ¾
- Medium celery ribs, 2
- Cloves of chopped garlic,3
- Dried oregano, 1 tbsp.
- Oregano to taste, and oil 1 tbsp.
- Bay leaves, 2
- Crushed cumin, 1 tsp.
- Chicken broth, 5 cups or enough to cover

Preparation/Procedure

1. Put pinto beans that have been soaked in a slow cooker. Add the ham, along with the celery, onion, bell pepper, onion, oregano, fat, cumin, and bay leaves. Give everything a generous amount of chicken broth to cover.

2. Cook beans on High for 5 to 6 hours, or until very soft.

Storage

Cover the container with a lid and store it in the refrigerator.

Reheating

Reheat it in the pan or microwave it for 2 minutes.

Nutritional facts/values (per serving)

Calories: 366 | Fat: 14g | Carbohydrates: 38g | Protein: 24g | Sodium: 1348mg | Potassium: 858mg | Sugar: 2g

8 VEGETABLE AND VEGETARIAN DISHES

8.1 Slow Cooker Root Vegetables

9 Servings | Preparation Time: 20 min | Cook Time: 200min

Ingredients/Food List

- Medium Carrots 6
- Medium parsnips 4
- Medium red onions 2
- Medium sweet potatoes 3 cups
- Honey 3 tbsp.
- Olive oil 1 tbsp.
- Thyme leaves 5 tsp.
- Salt 1tsp.
- Black pepper 1tsp.
- White vinegar 1tbsp.

Preparation/Procedure

1. Apply cooking spray to the slow cooker. Combine onions, parsnips, and carrots in a slow cooker. Add sweet potatoes on top.
2. Add honey, oil, 2 tbsp. of thyme, salt, and pepper in a small bowl. Stir well to coat the vegetables after pouring them over.
3. Cover; cook on Low heat setting for 4 to 5 hours. Add vinegar right before serving, and gently whisk. Add the final three tbsp. of thyme.

Storage

Cover the container with a lid and store it in the refrigerator or freezer for later use.

Reheating

Keep the vegetables at room temperature for a few minutes.

Nutritional Facts/Values (per serving)

Calories: 120 | Fat: 2g | Carbohydrates: 25g | Protein: 2g I Sodium: 310mg | Potassium: 241mg |Sugar: 63g

8.2 Slow Cooker Winter Vegetables with Coconut Milk and Asian Chilli Sauce

Servings 8 | Preparation Time: 10 min | Cook Time: 4 hours 10 min

Ingredients/Food List

- Butternut squash 48oz can
- Medium sweet potatoes 4
- Shiitake Mushrooms 10oz
- Scallions 1cup
- Coconut Milk 14oz
- Water 1 and ½ cups
- Soya Sauce 3tbsp.
- Asian chili paste 2tsp.
- Cilantro leaves 1 cup

- Kosher salt 1tsp.
- Salted Peanuts ¼ cup

Preparation/Procedure

1. In the slow cooker, combine the whites of the scallions, potatoes, shiitake mushrooms, and squash. In a bowl, combine the coconut milk, water, soy sauce, sambal, and salt. Pour the mixture over the vegetables. For 4 hours on HIGH, covered, or until tender.
2. Divide the vegetables and broth equally among the warm bowls. Serve atop the scallion leaves, cilantro, and peanuts.

Storage

Keep this stew in the refrigerator for later use.

Reheating

It is better to heat the stew on the stove for 3 to 4 min or place it in the oven for 1 minute.

Nutritional Facts/Value (Per Serving)

Calories: 583 | Fat: 24g | Carbohydrate: 89g | Protein: 11g | Sodium: 790g | Potassium: 880g | Sugar: 18g

8.3 Vegetable and Cheese Stew with Tortellini

Servings: 4 | Preparation Time: 15 min | Cook Time: 5 hours and 30 min

Ingredients/Food List

- Small yellow Zucchini 4
- Dried chervil 1/2tsp.
- Basil leaves 1/2tsp.
- Allspice 1/4tsp.
- Chopped onion 1/2cup
- Green bell pepper 1cup
- Sliced Mushrooms 1cup
- Canned stewed tomatoes 14Oz
- Vegetable broth can of 14Oz
- Cooked cheese tortellini 9Oz (1 package)
- Salt and pepper to taste

Preparation/Procedure

1. In a slow cooker, combine all the ingredients (apart from the zucchini, salt, and tortellini); cover and cook on high for 4 to 5 hours, adding the zucchini for the last 30 minutes.

2. Sprinkle salt and pepper over the tortellini in shallow bowls, to taste.

Storage

Place the leftover recipe in a box, secure the lid, and put the box in the refrigerator or freezer.

Reheating

Take the required quantity from the refrigerator, heat in the microwave for 1 minute, and serve.

Nutritional Facts/Values (Per Serving)

Calories: 276 | Fat: 5g | Carbohydrate: 47g | Protein: 13g | Sodium: 511mg | Sugar: 3g | Potassium: 783g

8.4 Slow-Cooker Lentil Soup

Servings: 8 | Preparation Time: 30 min | Cook Time: 6 hours and 30 min

Ingredients/Food List

- Butternut squash 2 cups
- Chopped carrots and potatoes 2 cups
- Minced garlic 5 cloves
- Vegetable broth 8 cups
- Green lentils 1cup
- Split peas ¾ cup
- Medium chopped onion 1
- Chopped celery 2 cup
- Herbs de Provence (Thyme, oregano, summer savory, and rosemary)
- Salt and red wine vinegar 1 tsp. each
- Olive oil ½ cup
- Parsley 1 cup
- Kale 2 cup

Preparation/Procedure

1. Put all the ingredients in the slow cooker. Cook covered for 5–6 hours on high or 7-8 hours on low.
2. Blend the olive oil and about 4 cups of soup in a blender. Gently pulse until the mixture resembles a semi-creamy texture (the oil will form a creamy emulsion with the soup). Stir to blend after adding back to the saucepan.
3. Add the parsley and kale after that. Just turn off the heat and wait a little while for everything to cool before serving.
4. Serve with crusty wheat bread to take it to the next level and season to taste (at this point, add red wine vinegar).

Storage

For subsequent usage, store the vegetables with a lid in the refrigerator.

Reheating

Heat the leftover lentil soup in the microwave for 2-3 minutes.

Nutritional Facts/Values (Per Serving)

Calories: 319 | Fat: 15g | Carbohydrate: 39g | Protein: 11g | Sodium: 768mg | Sugar: 6.5g | Potassium: 819mg

8.5 Vegan Pumpkin Spice Trail Mix

Servings: 6 | Preparation Time: 10 min | Cook Time: 1 hour

Ingredients/Food List

- Walnut halves 2 and ¼ cup
- Cashews 1/3 cup
- Pumpkin Seeds ½ cup
- Chopped pecans 1/3 cup
- Dried cranberries 1 cup
- Chocolate chips ¾ cup

- Pumpkin spice 1 tbsp.
- Vanilla extract 1 tsp.
- Coconut oil 2tbsp.
- Coconut sugar ¼ cup
- Pinch of sea salt

Preparation/Procedure

1. In the slow cooker put the nuts and seeds, salt, coconut oil, sugar, and spices should all be added, and everything should be thoroughly mixed and coated.
2. If your nuts require more time to "roast," cover and leave on high for 90 minutes instead of an hour. Don't forget to stir once or twice while cooking.
3. Remove the nuts from the slow cooker when you believe they are sufficiently toasted and spread them out in an even layer on parchment paper.
4. After letting the mixture dry, move it to a mixing bowl. Stir in the chocolate and cranberries after adding them and serve.

Storage

Keep it in an airtight container or plastic bag with a zip top and place it in the refrigerator.

Reheating

Take the desired quantity from the plastic bag and heat it in the microwave.

Nutritional Facts/Values (Per Serving)

Calories: 129 | Fat: 9g | Carbohydrates: 12g | Protein: 2g | Sodium: 2mg | Sugar: 9g | Potassium: 3.5mg

8.6 Slow Cooker Vegetarian Minestrone Soup

6 Servings | Preparation Time: 20 min | Cook Time: 6 hours 30 min

Ingredients/Food List

- Dried Cannellini beans 8Oz
- Medium Carrots 3
- Garlic Cloves 3
- Bay leaves 2
- Sweet potato 1
- Large stalks of celery 2
- Medium yellow onion 1
- Crushed red pepper flakes 1/4tsp.
- Crushed tomatoes 28Oz can
- Diced tomatoes 28Oz can
- Tomato paste 3tbsp.
- Kale 2cup
- Kosher salt 1tbsp.
- Black pepper 2tsp.

Preparation/Procedure

1. Add the beans, carrots, garlic, bay leaves, celery, sweet potato, onion, crushed red pepper flakes, 1 tbsp. salt, and a few grinds of black pepper. Add the tomato paste, chopped tomatoes, crushed tomatoes, and 4 cups water by stirring. Cook with the lid on for 6 hours on high or 8 hours on low.
2. Add the kale, stir, then cook for 10 minutes with the lid on. Pour the soup into dishes.

Storage

Keep the vegetables with a lid in the refrigerator for later use.

Reheating

Keep the vegetables in the oven for one minute or keep them at room temperature for 10-15 minutes.

Nutritional Facts/Values (per serving)

Calories: 360 | Fat: 2g |Carbohydrate: 72g | Protein: 18g | Sodium: 1149mg | Potassium: 289mg | Sugar 16g.

8.7 Vegetarian Chilli

Servings 6 | Preparation Time: 15 min | Cook Time: 6 hours 15 min

Ingredients/Food List

- Canned tomatoes 28Oz
- Vegetable broth 4cup
- Black, red and white beans 15Oz can
- Chopped onion 1cup
- Medium green bell pepper 1
- Minced pickled jalapeno 1 tbsp.
- Chili powder and dried oregano 2tbsp.
- Hot sauce 2tsp.
- Couscous 1/3 cup
- Monterey jack cheese 1/2cup
- Salt, black pepper and cilantro leaves

Preparation/Procedure

1. Combine all of the ingredients in a slow cooker, excluding the couscous, shredded cheese, cilantro, salt, and pepper. Cook covered for 7 hours on low or 3.5 hours on high.
2. Add the couscous five to ten minutes before serving, cover, and cook until the couscous is cooked. Sprinkle on salt and black pepper, to taste. Top each plate with fresh cilantro leaves and shredded cheese right before serving.

Storage

Place the leftover in a container and cover it with a lid, place the container in the refrigerator.

Reheating

Take the quantity you need out of the fridge, reheat it in the microwave or on a pan, and then serve.

Nutritional Facts/Values (Per Serving)

Calories: 377| Fat: 6g | Carbohydrate: 64g | Protein: 22g | Sodium: 1353mg | Sugar: 9g | Potassium: 567mg

8.8 Spicy Peanut Soup with Sweet Potato and Kale

Servings: 6 |Preparation Time: 25 min | Cook Time: 5 hours and 30 min

Ingredients/Food List

- Olive oil 2tbsp.
- Diced Onion half
- Minced garlic cloves 2
- Minced jalapeno 1
- Cubed sweet potatoes 3
- Canned tomatoes 14Oz

- Water 2cup
- Salt and turmeric 1tsp. each
- Chopped peanuts ½ cup
- Chopped kale 2 cup
- Peanut butter ¼ cup

Preparation/Procedure

1. On low for 5 hours, cook everything except peanut butter and greens.
2. Add the greens and peanut butter after that.
3. Add the sweet potatoes just 15 min before serving because they will fall apart if you overcook them. Just heat them until a fork easily pierces them.
4. Topped with peanuts and serve.

Storage

Refrigerate the leftover recipe after storing in it and covering it with a lid.

Reheating

Take the quantity you need out of the fridge, reheat it in a pan, and then serve. It is better to not reheat the soup in the microwave.

Nutritional Facts/Values (Per Serving)

Calories: 288 | Fat: 20g | Carbohydrate: 23g | Protein: 6.5g | Sodium: 558mg | Sugar: 8g | Potassium: 533mg

8.9 Slow Cooker Ratatouille Briam

Servings: 8 | Preparation Time: 30 min | Cook Time: 2 hours and 30 min

Ingredients/Food List

- Sliced onion 1
- Sliced garlic cloves 4-5
- Extra virgin olive oil 3 tbsp.
- Crushed Tomato paste 2 tbsp.
- Medium Zucchini 2
- Large eggplant 1
- Bell pepper 1
- Chopped fresh thyme leaves 1 tbsp.
- Greek oregano
- Salt 1 and ½ tsp.
- Black pepper ¼ tsp.
- Medium plum tomatoes 5

Preparation/Procedure

1. In a sink, toss the eggplant with 1 teaspoon of salt. After 30 minutes of resting, the eggplant is drained and rinsed with cold water. To absorb as much moisture as possible, place the eggplant on paper towels and pat it with additional paper towels.
2. Combine the black pepper, remaining 1/2 teaspoon of salt, oil, and tomato paste, in a medium bowl.
3. Combine the drained and rinsed eggplant, thyme, garlic, onion, bell pepper, zucchini, and tomatoes in a slow cooker. After adding the oil-tomato paste mixture, stir it in.
4. Cover the pot and cook the vegetables on LOW for four hours, or until they are tender. Then, uncover the pan and continue cooking for an additional hour to allow some of the liquid to evaporate and the veggies to combine further.

Storage

Store in an air-tight container and cover it with a lid. Place the container in the refrigerator.

Reheating

Take the desired quantity from the refrigerator and heat it in the microwave oven.

Nutritional Facts/Values (Per Serving)

Calories: 130 | Fat: 8g | Carbohydrate: 15g | Protein: 3g | Sodium: 280mg | Sugar: 9g | Potassium: 313mg

8.10 Eggplant Curry

Servings: 4 | Preparation time: 15 min | Cook Time: 5 hours

Ingredients/Food List

- Peeled and chopped eggplant 4 cup
- Chopped Zucchini 4 cup
- Medium chopped onion
- Garlic cloves 4
- Curry Powder 1tbsp.
- Garam Masala 1tbsp.
- Black pepper ¼ tsp.
- Cumin ¼ tsp.
- Salt 1tsp.
- Tomato paste 6Oz can
- Coconut Milk 15Oz can
- Fresh parsley
- Vegetable broth ¼ cup

Preparation/Procedure

1. To your slow cooker, add onion, garlic, eggplant, zucchini, spices, tomato paste, and coconut milk. Combine all of the ingredients. If the mixture appears too thick at this point, you can add some vegetable broth.
2. Cook for 4-5 hours on low. Add fresh cilantro or parsley as a garnish. Warm up and serve with naan and rice.

Storage

Place the leftover curry in a container and cover it with a lid and place it in the refrigerator.

Reheating

Take the quantity needed from the container and place it in the oven for 1 minute.

Nutritional Facts/Values (Per Serving)

Calories:253 | Fat: 15g | Carbohydrates: 28g | Protein: 7g | Sodium: 677mg | Sugar: 16g | Potassium: 1140mg.

8.11 Vegetable Curry with Chickpeas

Servings: 4 | Preparation Time: 10 min | Cook Time 8 hours

Ingredients/Food List

- Cauliflower 4 cup
- Brussels sprouts 2 cup

- Peeled and diced sweet potato 1
- Drained chickpeas 15oz
- Tomato Sauce 15oz
- Vegetable broth ½ cup
- Cumin, turmeric, and curry powder 1tbsp. each
- Medium onion 1
- Green peas ½ cup
- Light Coconut milk ½ cup
- Diced red pepper 1
- Salt and black pepper to taste
- Plain Yogurt

Preparation/Procedure

1. Place the following ingredients in the slow cooker: veggies, chickpeas, tomato sauce, coconut milk, chicken broth, and spices. Cook on Low for 8 hours or on High for 4 hours.
2. Green peas are heated and added just before serving. Seasoning should be checked, and adjustments made.
3. Serve the yogurt, cilantro, and scallions with the grain of your choice, over brown rice, or on its own.

Storage

Keep the leftover curry in a container, cover it with a lid, and place it in the refrigerator.

Reheating

Take the desired quantity in a bowl and heat it in the oven for 1 minute.

Nutritional Facts/Values (Per Serving

Calories: 292 | Fat: 5g | Carbohydrate: 55g | Protein: 13g | Sodium: 912mg | Sugar: 16g | Potassium: 990mg

8.12 Sweet Potato and Spinach Curry

Servings: 4 | Preparation Time: 10 min | Cook Time: 3 hours

Ingredients/Food List

- Cubed and frozen sweet potatoes 20Oz
- Frozen cut spinach 1cup
- Sliced onions ½ cup
- Salt ½ tsp.
- Ginger powder ½ tsp.
- Red curry paste 3 tbsp.
- Lemon juice 2 tbsp.
- Vegetable broth ½ cup
- Canned coconut milk 14 Oz

Preparation/Procedure

1. To a slow cooker, add all ingredients except lime juice.
2. To blend, stir. Cook covered for 2-4 hours on high or 4-6 hours on low.
3. Stir in the lime juice after adding it.
4. Serve with fresh cilantro on top of the steaming white rice, or whatever you like.

Storage

Store the leftover curry in a container and cover it with a lid. Place it in a refrigerator.

Reheating

Take the quantity needed from the container and heat it in the microwave for 1 minute.

Nutritional Facts/Values (Per Serving)

Calories: 387 | Fat: 25g | Carbohydrates: 40g | Protein: 6g | Sodium: 531mg | Potassium: 915mg | Sugar:12g

8.13 Slow cooked Creamy Broccoli

Servings: 10 | Preparation Time: 10 min | Cook Time: 3 hours

Ingredients/Food List

- Frozen chopped broccoli 6 cup
- Condensed cream of celery soup, undiluted 10Oz can
- Shredded cheddar cheese 1 and ½ cups
- Worcestershire sauce ½ tsp.
- Chopped onion ¼ cup
- Black pepper ¼ tsp.
- Butter 2 tbsp.
- Crushed butter-flavored crackers 1 cup

Preparation/Procedure

1. Broccoli, soup, 1 cup cheese, onion, Worcestershire sauce, and pepper should all be combined in a big bowl.
2. Fill a 3-quart slow cooker with cooking oil. Top with crackers and butter, then sprinkle.
3. Cook for 2-1/2 to 3 hours with a cover on high.
4. Add the remaining cheese on top. Cook for 10 minutes more, or until the cheese has melted.

Storage

Store the leftover broccoli in a container with a lid and place that container in the refrigerator.

Reheating

Take the desired quantity from the refrigerator and heat it in the microwave for 1 minute.

Nutritional Facts/Values (Per Serving)

Calories: 159 | Fat: 11g | Carbohydrate: 11g | Protein: 6g | Sodium: 431mg | Sugar: 2g | Potassium: 287mg

8.14 Slow Cooker Butternut Squash with Whole Grains

Servings: 12 | Preparation Time: 15 min | Cook Time: 4 hours

Ingredients/Food List

- Medium cubed butternut squash 1
- Brown and red rice blend 1 cup
- Chopped medium onion 1
- Minced garlic cloves 3
- Water ½ cup
- Salt ½ tsp.
- Black pepper ¼ tsp.
- Fresh chopped thyme 2 tsp.
- Fresh baby spinach 6oz
- Vegetable Broth 14oz can

Preparation/Procedure

1. Combine the first 8 ingredients in a 4-qt slow cooker. Mix in the broth.
2. Cook the grains for 4-5 hours on low, covered, until they are soft. Before serving, incorporate spinach.

Storage

Store the leftover recipe in a container, cover it with a lid and place it in the refrigerator.

Reheating

Take the required quantity from the refrigerator and heat it in the microwave oven for 1 minute.

Nutritional facts/Values (Per Serving)

Calories: 97 | Fat: 1g | Carbohydrates: 22g | Protein: 3g | Sodium: 252mg | Potassium: 291mg | Sugar: 3g

8.15 Slow Cooker Spinach Marinara Sauce

Servings: 8 | Preparation Time: 15 min | Cook Time: 3 hours

Ingredients/Food List

- Olive oil ¼ cup
- Medium chopped onion 1
- Grated carrot 1/3 cup
- Minced garlic cloves 5
- Freshly chopped spinach 10Oz
- Canned tomato paste 6Oz (2 cans)
- Dried oregano 2 tbsp.
- Dried basil 2 tbsp.
- Basil 2 tbsp.
- Crushed red pepper 2 and ½ tbsp.
- Canned tomatoes with liquid 28Oz can
- Bay leaves 2

Preparation/Procedure

1. Olive oil, onion, garlic, carrot, spinach, tomato paste, mushrooms, salt, oregano, basil, crushed red pepper, bay leaves, and tomatoes should all be combined in a 5-quart slow cooker.
2. For four hours, cook covered on high. Stir, lower heat to low, and simmer for a further one to two hours.

Storage

Store the leftover recipe in a container with a lid and place it in the refrigerator for later use.

Reheating

Take the desired quantity from the container and heat it in the microwave for 1 minute.

Nutritional Facts/Values (Per Serving)

Calories: 86 | Fat: 7g | Carbohydrates: 5g | Protein: 2g | Sodium: 1757mg | Sugar: 2g | Potassium: 201mg

8.16 Vegetable stuffed peppers

Servings:4 | Preparation Time: 15 min | Cook Time: 3 hours 10 min

Ingredients/Food List

- 4 large bell peppers (Any colour)
- Cooked quinoa 2 cup
- Corn kernels 1 cup

- Drained black beans 15oz can
- Large avocado 1
- Water
- Lime wedges
- Hot sauce ½ tsp.
- Cilantro leaves chopped ½ cup
- Salt ¼ tsp.
- Lemon juice 2tsp.
- Garlic salt ½ tsp.
- Smoked paprika ½ tsp.
- Chili powder 1tsp.

Preparation/Procedure

1. Mix quinoa, corn kernels, black beans, chili powder, paprika, garlic salt, and salt thoroughly in a big bowl.
2. The quinoa mixture should be placed inside each pepper half. Cook the pepper halves in the slow cooker for three hours on high.
3. Prepare the avocado topping while the peppers are cooking. In a bowl, thoroughly mash the avocado. Stir in the salt, spicy sauce, and lime juice until the mixture is extremely smooth. Add just enough water to make it as thin as you like (start with a teaspoon or so).
4. Avocado sauce, chopped cilantro, and lime wedges should be served with peppers.

Storage

Store the stuffed peppers in a container with a lid and place the container in the refrigerator.

Reheating

Take the required quantity from the container and heat it in the microwave or on a pan and serve.

Nutritional Facts/Values (Per Serving)

Calories: 471 | Fat: 13g | Carbohydrate: 76g | Protein: 18g | Sodium: 1626mg | Sugar: 16g | Potassium: 1717g

8.17 Burrito Bowls

Servings: 4 | Preparation Time: 10 min | Cook Time: 3 hours

Ingredients/Food List

- Diced green bell pepper and red chilli 1
- Black beans 1 and ¼ cup
- Brown rice 1 cup
- Chopped Tomatoes 1 and ½ cups
- Chipotle hot sauce 1tbsp.
- Smoked paprika 1tsp.
- Ground cumin ½ tsp.
- Salt and black pepper to taste
- Grated cheese of your choice to serve
- Fresh cilantro leaves

Preparation/Procedure

1. The ingredients for the burrito bowl (except the toppings) should all be added to a slow cooker. Mix well.
2. Cook the rice on low for approximately 3 hours, or until it is done. Try cooking rice on high if your rice doesn't cook properly on low setting.

3. Serve hot and garnish as desired.

Storage

Store the leftover recipe in a container with a lid on it and place it in the refrigerator for later use.

Reheating

Take the required quantity from the container and heat it in the microwave oven for 1 minute.

Nutritional Facts/Values (Per Serving)

Calories: 389 | Fat: 3g | Carbohydrates: 80g | Protein: 12g | Sodium: 216mg | Potassium: 1013mg | Sugar: 6g

8.18 Slow Cooker Spring Veggies

Servings: 8 | Preparation Time: 10 min | Cook Time: 4 hours

Ingredients/Food List

- Large onion 1
- Medium Carrots 4
- Red potatoes 2 cup
- Melted butter 3 tbsp.
- Frozen peas 1 cup
- Grated lemon zest 1 tsp.
- Fresh chives ¼ cup
- Salt and black pepper ¼ tsp. each

Preparation/Procedure

1. In a 4-qt. slow cooker, combine the carrots, onion, and potatoes. Add salt and pepper, then drizzle with melted butter. Cook covered on low for 4-5 hours, or until vegetables are soft.
2. To the slow cooker, add peas. Cook for 10-15 minutes on high, covered, until well heated. Add lemon zest and stir. Sprinkle chives on top.

Storage

Store the vegetables in a container with a lid and place it in the refrigerator.

Reheating

Take the desired quantity from the container and heat it in the microwave for 1 minute.

Nutritional Facts/Values (Per Serving)

Calories: 141 | Fat: 5g | Carbohydrate: 3g | Protein: 3g | Sodium: 298mg | Sugar: 5g | Potassium: 340mg

8.19 Slow Cooker Turnip Greens

Servings: 10 | Preparation Time: 30 min | Cook Time: 5 hours

Ingredients/Food List

- Cubed medium turnips 3
- Fresh turnip greens 2 cups
- Olive oil 2 tbsp.
- Granulated sugar 1 tbsp.
- Red pepper flakes 1 tsp.

Preparation/Procedure

1. Spray non-stick cooking spray on the slow cooker's insert.

2. Half of the greens, 1 cup of water, turnips that have been peeled and quartered, and olive oil should all be added to the slow cooker. Add the sugar and red pepper flakes if you're using them.

3. Greens should be lowered after about an hour of cooking on low. The slow cooker should now contain all of the greens. Set the timer for 4 more hours on low. The flavor of turnip greens improves with cooking time.

Storage

Store the leftover turnip greens in a container with a lid on it, and place the container in the refrigerator.

Reheating

Take the required quantity from the container and heat it in the microwave for 1 minute.

Nutritional Facts/Values (Per Serving)

Calories: 127 | Fat: 1g | Carbohydrates: 28g | Protein: 6g | Sodium: 170mg | Potassium: 1144mg | Sugar: 4g

8.20 Slow Cooker Low Carb Lasagna

Servings: 6 | Preparation Time: 30 min | Cook Time: 2 hours 30 min

Ingredients/Food List

- Medium red onion 1
- Red bell pepper 1
- Medium eggplant 1
- Medium zucchini 2
- Tomato-based pasta sauce 2 cup
- Low-fat cottage cheese 16Oz
- Skimmed and shredded mozzarella cheese 8 oz
- Large eggs 2
- Salt to taste
- Parmesan cheese for serving
- Freshly chopped basil or parsley

Preparation/Procedure

1. Slice the eggplant and zucchini lengthwise into long, thin strips, resembling lasagna noodles, using an extremely sharp knife.

2. The vegetable slices should be spread out on a kitchen towel and kosher salt should be lightly sprinkled over them. 15 minutes of standing time will help some of the extra liquid drain off. Clean off.

3. Set a grill pan indoors or outside to medium heat. Grill the eggplant and zucchini strips for two to three minutes on each side, turning once, until cooked through and lightly browned.

4. Spray some non stick cooking spray in a 6-quart crock pot lightly. The layer of tomato sauce in the bottom of the slow cooker should be about 1/2 cup. Beat the eggs and cottage cheese together in a small bowl.

5. In a slow cooker, prepare the first layer of lasagna as follows: 1 layer of eggplant, 1/3 cup of cottage cheese, 1/3 cup of bell peppers and onions, 1/3 cup of mozzarella, and 1/2 cup of tomato sauce.

6. Make the second layer of the vegetable lasagna, using zucchini this time: 1 layer of zucchini, 1/3 cup of tomato sauce, 1/3 of the cottage cheese, 1/3 of the bell peppers, onions, and mozzarella.

7. Make the last layer: 1 layer of zucchini noodles; 1/2 cup tomato sauce; remaining mozzarella; 1 layer of eggplant, remaining bell peppers and onions; and 1 layer of remaining cottage cheese.

8. When the eggplant is soft, simmer it for 2 to 3 hours on high in a covered crock pot. To see if the eggplant is soft, insert a long, thin knife into the lasagna. Recover, shut off the slow cooker, and allow stand for 30 to 60 minutes or until any liquid is absorbed.

9. Slice and scoop pieces as desired, then top with desired amounts of Parmesan cheese and seasonings.

Storage

Store the leftover lasagna in a container and cover it with a lid. Place the container in the refrigerator.

Reheating

Take the desired quantity from the container and heat it in the microwave.

Nutritional Facts/Values (Per Serving)

Calories: 273 | Fat: 12g | Carbohydrates: 22g | Protein: 23g | Sodium: 963mg | Sugar: 12g | Potassium: 1024mg

9 BEEF, PORK AND LAMB RECIPES

9.1 Slow Cooker Beef Sloppy Joes

Servings: 6 | Preparation Time: 10 min | Cook Time: 3 hours

Ingredients/Food List

- Grounded beef 4 cups
- Tomato sauce 8Oz (2cans)
- Hamburger buns 6
- Diced onions and ketchup ½ cup each
- Worcestershire sauce 2 tsp.
- Vegetable oil 2 tsp.
- Brown sugar 2tbsp.
- Garlic powder ½ tsp.
- Salt and pepper to taste

Preparation/Procedure

1. In a big pan, heat the oil on medium-high.
2. Add salt and pepper to taste and then add the ground meat to the pan. Cook the beef while breaking it up with a spatula for 6 to 8 minutes.
3. Cook for an additional 4-5 minutes after adding the onion.
4. Put the tomato sauce, ketchup, brown sugar, Worcestershire sauce, garlic powder, 1/2 teaspoon salt, and 1/4 teaspoon pepper in the slow cooker with the beef and onion combination.
5. Combine the ingredients by stirring.
6. LOW for six hours or HIGH for three hours.
7. Serve the meat by spooning it onto the hamburger buns.

Storage

Store the leftover ground beef in a container with a lid on it and place it in the refrigerator.

Reheating

Reheat the desired quantity of beef from the container in a large pan or microwave for 1 minute.

Nutritional Facts/Values (Per Serving)

Calories: 376 | Fat: 14g | Carbohydrates: 32g | Protein 27g |Sodium: 494mg | Potassium: 517mg | Sugar: 11g

9.2 Slow Cooker Corned Beef

Servings: 8 | Preparation time: 10 min | Cook Time: 8 hours

Ingredients/Food List

- Uncooked corned silverside beef 2.5kg
- Whole peppercorns 10
- Water 4cup
- Chopped medium brown onion 1
- Brown sugar 2tbsp.
- Bay Leaves 2

Preparation/Procedure

1. Fill the bowl of a 5-liter slow cooker with silverside (a 2.5 kg chunk of uncooked corned silverside, fat removed, washed). the rest of the ingredients.

2. Put a cover on top. Set the slow cooker to low. Until the silverside is soft, cook for 8 hours. Include roasted potatoes and steamed Brussels sprouts in the meal.

Storage

The leftover corned beef should be stored in the fridge in a jar with a lid.

Reheating

Use a large pan or microwave to reheat the desired quantity of beef from the container for one minute.

Nutritional Facts/Values (Per Serving)

Calories: 414 | Fat: 19g | carbohydrates: 5g | Protein: 56g | Sodium: 816mg | Potassium: 40mg | Sugar: 4g

9.3 Slow Cooker Pork loin

Servings: 8 | Preparation Time: 1o min | Cook Time: 6 hours

Ingredients/Food list

- Pork Loin 1
- Sliced round onions
- Chopped garlic cloves 4
- Oil 1tbsp.
- Soy sauce 2tbsp.
- Balsamic vinegar ½ cup
- Water ½ cup
- Brown sugar ½ cup

Preparation/Procedure

1. Salt and pepper the pork loin roast well on all sides. In the bottom of the slow cooker, add sliced onions. A big skillet should be heated at medium-high. Pork loin is added to the oil and seared for 2 minutes on each side, or until golden brown.

2. Remove from pan and set in slow cooker on top of onions.

3. Add the water, soy sauce, balsamic vinegar, and garlic to the skillet after turning off the heat. Mix the ingredients thoroughly.

4. Before pouring the sauce mixture over the pork loin, sprinkle brown sugar over the top of the meat.

5. To cook on Low for 5 to 6 hours or until the internal temperature reaches 145 degrees Fahrenheit, cover the pan and cook.

6. Remove the cooked pork loin to a platter, then wrap it in foil. Give yourself 10 minutes to rest.

7. Pour the sauce and fluids from the slow cooker into a saucepan while the pork is resting. Over medium heat, bring to a simmer and let the sauce sit for 5 to 6 minutes to thicken and stir.

Storage

The shelf life of leftovers is up to 3 days in the refrigerator or 3 months in the freezer

Reheating

Take the desired quantity of pork loin from the container and heat it in the microwave for 2 minutes.

Nutritional Facts/Values (Per Serving)

Calories: 240 | Fat: 8g | Carbohydrates: 12g | Protein: 33g | Sodium: 352mg | Potassium: 870mg | Sugar: 8g

9.4 Pork with Sauerkraut and Potatoes

Servings: 4 | Preparation Time: 10 min | Cook Time: 8 hours

Ingredients/Food List

- Whole pork tenderloin 1
- Unpeeled baby potatoes 24Oz
- Sauerkraut 20Oz can
- Water 1 cup
- Cubed butter ¼ cup
- Salt and black pepper to taste

Preparation/Procedure

1. Put a slow cooker with a whole pork tenderloin inside. Place potatoes around the pig, then top with sauerkraut and juice. Butter cubes, salt, black pepper, and 1 cup of water are added.
2. Cook the pork for 8 to 10 hours on low to make it tender. If the mixture seems dry after eight hours, add more water.

Storage

In the refrigerator or freezer, leftovers can be stored for up to 3 days.

Reheating

The leftover recipe should be heated in the microwave for two minutes after being removed from the container in the desired amount.

Nutritional Facts/Values (Per Serving)

Calories: 358 | Fat: 15g | Carbohydrates: 36g | Protein: 22g | Sodium: 1057mg | Potassium: 1240mg | Sugar: 4g

9.5 Slow Cooker Lamb Shanks with Tomatoes

Servings: 6 | Preparation Time: 15 min | Cook Time: 6 hours

Ingredients/Food List

- Lamb Shanks 6
- Massel beef style liquid stock 1 cup
- Rosemary 1tbsp.
- Tomato pesto 2tbsp.
- Diced canned tomatoes 3 and ½ cups
- Tomato paste 2 tbsp.
- Diced onion 1
- Garlic cloves 4
- Olive oil 1 tsp.

Preparation/Procedure

1. In a small saucepan, heat the olive oil over medium heat before adding the onion. Stir until transparent onion is achieved.
2. Cook for a further three minutes after adding the garlic.
3. Cook for an additional two minutes after stirring in the tomato paste.
4. Add beef stock, sundried tomato pesto, and diced tomatoes. Heat should be turned off after stirring thoroughly and bringing it to a boil.
5. Lamb and rosemary leaves should be placed in the slow cooker, and tomato sauce should be added on top.
6. Cook for eight hours on low.

7. Traditional oven Set the oven to 170 °C (fan-forced 150 °C).
8. In a casserole dish, combine the lamb with the rosemary leaves. Cover with tomato sauce. Cook for two hours in the oven with a lid on the dish.

Storage
Store the leftover recipe in a container with a lid on it and place it in the refrigerator.

Reheating
Take the desired quantity from the container and heat the shanks in a pan on low flame or in the microwave for 2 to 3 minutes.

Nutritional Facts/Values (Per Serving)
Calories: 185 | Fat: 12g | Carbohydrates: 1g | Protein: 19g | Sodium: 77mg | Sugar: 1g | Potassium: 145mg

9.6 Barbecue Pork Ribs

Servings: 6 | Preparation Time: 10 min | Cook Time 3 hours

Ingredients/Food List
- Barbecue Sauce 2 cup
- Brown Sugar 2 tbsp.
- Worcestershire sauce 2tsp.
- Minced Garlic 3tbsp.
- Cayenne Pepper 1tbsp.
- Baby pork ribs 2kg
- Salt and Black Pepper to taste

Preparation/Procedure
1. Apply cooking spray to the interior of a 6-quart slow cooker.
2. Put the ribs in the slow cooker after removing the inner skin (membrane). Throw away skin.
3. In a small bowl, mix the cayenne pepper, barbecue sauce, brown sugar, Worcestershire sauce, and garlic. Add half of the sauce, mix well to blend, and completely cover.
4. Add a generous amount of pepper and salt to the dish, cover it with a lid, and cook it for 7-9 hours on low or 3-5 hours on high in the oven. Keep any leftover sauce in the fridge for later use.
5. When the ribs are cooked and coming apart, place them on a parchment-lined oven tray (or baking sheet).
6. Pour half of the slow cooker fluids into the remaining sauce. Broil (grill) the ribs in a preheated oven at 400°F (220°C) for about 10 minutes, basting with half of the sauce.
7. Serve ribs with the remaining sauce.

Storage
Store the leftover barbecue ribs in the container and place them in the refrigerator.

Reheating
Take the required quantity from the container and heat it in the microwave for 2 minutes.

Nutritional Facts/Values (Per Serving)
Calories: 624 | Fat: 38g | Carbohydrate: 38g | Protein: 59g | Sodium: 411mg | Potassium: 644mg | Sugar: 35g

9.7 Thai Style Peanut Pork

Servings: 8 | Preparation Time: 10 min | Cook Time: 8 hours

Ingredients/Food List

- Boneless pork chops 4 (8Oz)
- Rice vinegar 2tbsp.
- Sliced red bell peppers 2
- Teriyaki Sauce ½ cup
- Chopped green onions ½ cup
- Creamy peanut butter ¼ cup
- Chopped roasted peanuts ¼ cup
- Lime wedges 2
- Minced garlic cloves 2
- Crushed red pepper flakes 1tsp.

Preparation/Procedure

1. Spray some cooking oil onto a slow cooker. Pork chops and bell pepper strips should be added to the slow cooker. Over the pork chops, mix the teriyaki sauce, vinegar, garlic, and red pepper flakes.

2. Pork should be cooked on Low for 8 to 9 hours with the cover on. Remove the pork from the slow cooker when it is done, then stir in the peanut butter until it is smooth. Cook the pork for a further 10 minutes in the slow cooker.

3. Pour into a serving dish, then top with peanuts and green onions for decoration. To serve, garnish with lime wedges.

Storage

Store the leftover recipe in a container with a lid on it and place it in the refrigerator.

Reheating

Take the desired quantity from the container and heat it in the microwave for 1 minute.

Nutritional Facts/Values (Per Serving)

Calories: 209 | Fat: 11g | Carbohydrate: 10g | Protein: 19g | Sodium: 788mg | Potassium: 439mg | Sugar: 5g

9.8 Easy Slow Cooker Lamb Stew

Servings: 6 | Preparation Time: 20 min | Cook Time: 8 hours

Ingredients/Food List

- Lamb shoulder 4 cups
- Beef broth 2 cups
- Minced garlic cloves 4
- Medium yellow onion 1
- Red wine 1 and ½ cups
- All-purpose flour ¼ cup
- Bay leaves 2
- Worcestshire sauce 2tbsp.
- Medium carrots 3
- FrOzen sweet peas 1 cup

- Chopped celery
- Baby mushrooms and red potatoes 2 cups
- Salt, black pepper, and fresh rosemary 1 tsp. each

Preparation/Procedure

1. Toss the flour, salt, and pepper with the lamb in a sizable basin. Add the olive oil to a big skillet and heat it over medium heat.
2. The lamb meat should be browned for around 3-5 minutes on each side until the oil is shimmering. Work may need to be done in batches. Although browning the pork is optional, recommending it since it preserves the flavor.
3. Except for the green peas, add all the ingredients to the slow cooker.
4. Cover and cook for 7-8 hours on low heat or 3-4 hours on high.
5. During the last hour of cooking, add the green peas.
6. Serve warm and garnish with freshly chopped parsley.

Storage

Store the leftover lamb stew in a container with a lid on it and place it in the refrigerator.

Reheating

Take the required quantity of lamb stew from the container and heat it in the microwave for 1 to 2 minutes.

Nutritional Facts/Values (Per Serving)

Calories: 656 | Fat: 37g | Carbohydrates: 37g | Protein: 33g | Sodium: 1190mg | Potassium: 1643mg | Sugar: 8g

9.9 Beef Pepper Steak

Servings: 6 | Preparation Time: 15 min | Cook Time: 5 hours

Ingredients/Food List

- Beef strips 4 cups
- Green, red bell pepper and onion 1 each
- Water ½ cup
- Beef bouillon cubes 2
- Soy sauce 3 tbsp.
- Corn starch 1tbsp.
- Brown sugar/honey 2tsp.
- Red pepper flakes ¼ tsp.
- Worcestershire sauce 1 tsp.
- Black pepper ½ tsp.
- Ginger and garlic powder ¼ tsp. each

Preparation/Procedure

1. Add the water and the beef bouillon cubes to a small microwave-safe bowl. 30 seconds in the microwave, stirring until dissolved. Smash the bouillon cubes with the back of a spoon. Boil your water on the stovetop if you don't have a microwave.
2. To the bowl containing the water and bouillon, add the soy sauce, Worchestershire sauce, ginger, garlic powder, pepper, brown sugar, and cornflour. Until smooth, whisk. (If desired, add the red pepper flakes.) Place the slow cooker with this mixture inside.
3. In the slow cooker, combine the beef, bell peppers, and onions with the sauce.

4. Cook for 5 hours on LOW with a cover.

Storage

Leftovers should be frozen for up to three months or refrigerated for up to three days.

Reheating

Reheat the beef steak in the microwave for just 2 minutes.

Nutritional Facts/values (Per Serving)

Calories: 421 | Fat: 1g | Carbohydrates: 8g | Protein: 28g | Sodium: 939mg | Potassium:552mg | Sugar: 4

9.10 Slow Cooker Beef Tacos

Servings: 8 | Preparation Time: 5 min | Cook Time: 2 hours and 30 min

Ingredients/Food List

- Grounded Beef: 4 cups
- Mexican-style diced tomatoes 14Oz can
- Taco seasoning homemade 4tbsp.

Preparation/Procedure

1. All ingredients should be added to a 6-quart slow cooker and mixed.
2. Cook for 2.5 hours on high or 4 hours on low.
3. To separate the chunks, stir the meat. If necessary, use paper towels to absorb the grease. Put the scoop into the taco shells using a slotted spoon.
4. For tacos, nachos, or a taco salad, serve right away.

Storage

Any taco meat that is left over should be placed in an airtight container and kept in the fridge for up to 4 days. Additionally, taco meat may be frOzen for up to three months.

Reheating

Heat the desired quantity of beef tacos in the microwave oven for 1 minute.

Nutritional Facts/Values (Per Serving)

Calories: 222 | Fat: 0g | Carbohydrates: 6g | Protein: 23g | Sodium: 793mg | Potassium: 431mg | Sugar: 3g

9.11 Tender Roasted Beef

Servings: 4 | Preparation Time: 15 min | Cook Time: 5 hours

Ingredients/Foods List

- Top round beef 1kg
- Beef stock 2 cups
- Corn flour 6tbsp.
- Tomato puree 3tbsp.
- Red wine 1cup
- Chopped carrots 2
- Sliced onions 1
- Salt and black pepper 1tsp. each
- Sugar 2tsp.
- Olive oil 1 tbsp.

Preparation/Procedure

1. Add the onions and carrots to the slow cooker, then add the 3 tbsp. of cornflour and stir to coat everything evenly. Season the beef generously with salt and pepper and a little oil. In a heated pan, brown the beef all over before adding it to the slow cooker.

2. Make sure the beef is mostly submerged in the liquid before adding the beef stock, red wine, tomato puree, and sugar. Cook for 5 hours on low or 3 hours on high. Once cooked, take the steak out of the slow cooker and keep it warm by covering it with foil. For up to 30 minutes, the beef should rest.

3. Add 3 tablespoons of cornflour to the slow cooker's remaining liquid and veggies to thicken the sauce (remove a little liquid, mix in the cornflour to make a paste, and mix it back into the gravy).

4. Slice the steak thinly with a sharp knife and generously cover it with red wine gravy when it's time to serve!

Storage

Store the leftover roasted beef in a container with a lid and place it in the refrigerator.

Reheating

Reheat the required quantity of roasted beef in a microwave for 2-3 minutes.

Nutritional Facts/Values (Per Serving)

Calories: 429 | Fat: 9g | Carbohydrates: 19g | Protein: 57g | Sodium: 1002mg | Potassium:1324mg | Sugar: 6g

9.12 Slow Cooker Pork Carnitas

Servings: 10 | Preparation Time: 10 min | Cook Time: 8 hours

Ingredients/Food List

- Boneless pork shoulder roast 1 (4 pounds)
- Chicken broth 2 cups
- Bay Leaves 2
- Ground cinnamon ¼ tsp.
- Grounded coriander ½ tsp.
- Dried oregano ½ tsp.
- Cumin, garlic powder, and salt 1 tsp. each

Preparation/Procedure

1. Pork should be covered in a mixture of cinnamon, cumin, oregano, coriander, salt, and garlic powder. Bay leaves should be put in the bottom of the slow cooker before adding the pork. Making sure not to rinse off the spice combination, pour chicken broth over the sides of the meat.

2. For a total of around 10 hours, simmer the pork covered on Low, flipping the meat every 5 hours.

3. Remove the pork from the slow cooker once it is tender and shred it with two forks. As needed, add cooking liquid to moisten the meat.

Storage

Store the leftover carnitas in a container and place it in the refrigerator for up to 3 days or freeze it for 3 months.

Reheating

Heat the required quantity of pork carnitas in the microwave for 2 to 3 minutes.

Nutritional Facts/Values (Per Serving)

Calories: 223 | Fat: 14g | Carbohydrates: 1g | Protein: 22g | Sodium: 474mg | Potassium: 290mg | Sugar: 0g

9.13 Beef Chilli with Mushrooms

Servings: 8 | Preparation Time: 15 min | Cook Time: 6 hours and 20 min

Ingredients/Food List

- Ground beef 2 cups
- Minced garlic cloves 4
- Chopped onion 1
- Tomato paste 2tbsp.
- Kidney beans 15Oz (2 cans)
- Crushed tomatoes 10Oz can
- Beer 1 cup
- Chilli powder 1tbsp.
- Ground cumin 1tsp.
- Dried oregano 1tsp.
- Paprika ½ tsp.
- Kosher salt and black pepper
- Shredded cheddar, Fritos, and green onions are optional for serving

Preparation/Procedure

1. A big skillet should be heated at medium-high. For about 3 minutes, add the beef and onion and simmer until the meat is evenly (but not too) browned. (It doesn't have to be fully cooked!) Add tomato paste after draining the fat.
2. Combine the beef mixture with the kidney beans, crushed tomatoes, beer, garlic, cumin, oregano, paprika, and cayenne in a sizable slow cooker. Add salt and pepper to taste.
3. Cook for six to eight hours on low. (It becomes more flavourful the longer it cooks in the slow cooker.)
4. Taste the dish to check for seasonings. If preferred, top heated dishes with cheese, Fritos, and green onions.

Storage

The beef chili leftovers should be put in the refrigerator in a container with a lid.

Reheating

Reheat the desired amount of beef from the container in a big pan or for one minute in the microwave.

Nutritional Facts/Values (Per serving)

Calories 273 | Fat: 8g | Carbohydrates: 333g | Protein: 19g | Sodium: 975mg | Potassium: 54mg| Sugar: 5g

9.14 Slow Cooker Shredded Beef

Servings: 8 | Preparation Time: 20 min | Cook Time: 8 hours

Ingredients/Food List

- Beef chuck roast 8cups
- Stewed Tomatoes 15Oz
- Sliced Jalapeno 1
- Chopped white onion 1 cup

- Beef broth 1 cup
- Cilantro ¼ cup
- Salt and cumin 1 tsp. each
- Black pepper ½ tsp.
- Cooking oil 2 tbsp.

Preparation/Procedure

1. On the stovetop, preheat a sizable skillet over medium-high heat. Add the cooking oil once it's hot, then brown the chuck roast all over. Chuck roast should be added to the slow cooker.
2. Once the onions are slightly browned, return them to the pan with a little more oil and continue to sauté until the meat in the slow cooker is covered. Other ingredients can be added to the slow cooker.
3. For 9–10 hours, cook covered on LOW heat.
4. Remove the meat from the oven, place it on a platter, and shred it. Throw away any fat.
5. Reintroduce the meat to the slow cooker in the reserved juice after removing the fat from the pot but before using the remaining cup of juice. Dispense and savour!

Storage

In the refrigerator, leftovers kept in an airtight container will last for up to 5 days. The leftovers can be frozen and kept for up to three months.

Reheating

When you're ready to reheat them, let the leftovers completely defrost before warming them on the stove (over medium-low heat). Take the desired quantity and heat it in the microwave for 2 minutes.

Nutritional Facts/Values (Per Serving)

Calories: 47 | Fat: 30g | Carbohydrates: 7g | Protein: 44g | Sodium: 595mg | Potassium: 913mg | Sugar: 3g

9.15 Saucy Slow Cooker Pork Chops

Servings: 5 | Preparation Time: 15 min | Cook time: 6 hours

Ingredients/Food List

- Boneless pork chops 5
- Sliced green bell peppers 2
- Sliced onion 1
- Olive oil 3 tbsp.
- Brown sugar ¼ cup
- Canned tomato sauce 8Oz
- Worcestershire sauce 2tsp.
- Corn starch 2tbsp.
- Salt 1 and ½ tsp.
- Apple cider vinegar 1 tbsp.

Preparation/Procedure

1. Pork chops should be cooked for about five minutes on each side in olive oil that has been heated to medium heat in a large skillet. Pork chops that have been browned should be added to a slow cooker along with green peppers and onions.
2. In a bowl, combine tomato sauce, brown sugar, vinegar, Worcestershire sauce, and salt. Pour sauce into the slow cooker and give the meat and veggies a little toss to coat.

3. Cook pork chops on Low for 6 to 8 hours or until tender. Transfer pork chops to a serving platter; tent with aluminium foil to keep warm. Whisk corn-starch into sauce until thickened; spoon sauce and vegetables over pork chops.

Storage

Store the leftover pork chops in a refrigerator for up to 3 days or 3 months in the freezer.

Reheating

Pork chops should be heated in the microwave for two minutes after being removed from the container in the desired amount.

Nutritional Facts/Values (Per Serving)

Calories: 321 | Fat: 15g | Carbohydrates: 21g | Protein: 25g | Sodium: 995mg | Potassium: 640mg | Sugar: 15g

9.16 Easy Slow Cooker Lamb Tagine

Servings: 8 | Preparation Time: 15 min | Cook Time: 3 hours

Ingredients/Food List

- Diced Lamb 2 cups
- Chickpeas 1 cup
- Beef stock 6flOz
- Diced brown onion 1
- Vegetable oil 2tbsp.
- Minced garlic cloves 4
- Grated ginger 1 tbsp.
- Ground coriander 1tbsp.
- Cumin ½ tbsp.
- Cinnamon ¼ tsp.
- Paprika 1tsp.
- Honey 1tbsp.
- Chopped tomatoes 2 and ½ cups
- Chopped dates ½ oz.

Preparation/Procedure

1. Olive or vegetable oil is used to brown the lamb on all sides. Take out onto a platter.
2. While scraping out any brown pieces, add the minced onion, garlic, and ginger and cook for about 2 minutes.
3. Add the chopped tomatoes, stock, and lamb to the slow cooker along with the onions, garlic, and spices. 3 hours of cooking on medium.
4. Add the honey, chopped apricots, and drained can of chickpeas after the lamb is fork-tender, and simmer for an additional 20 to 30 minutes.
5. Add the honey and lemon juice after that. To taste and season as necessary.
6. Divide into dishes and garnish with Greek yogurt, chopped pistachios or almonds, and fresh coriander. If you like, add some mint leaves.

Storage

Store the leftover lamb tagine In a container with a lid on it and place it in the refrigerator.

Reheating

Reheat the required amount of tagine in a microwave for 1 to 2 minutes or in a pan on the stove.

Nutritional Facts/Values (Per Serving)

Calories: 285 | Fat: 21g | Carbohydrates: 10g | Protein: 14g | Sodium: 168mg | Potassium: 393mg | Sugar: 7g

10 FISH AND SEA FOOD

10.1 Shrimp soup

6 Servings | Preparation time: 15 mins | Cook time: 180 mins

Ingredients/Food list

- Shrimp, 2 cups
- Tomatoes, cubed, 1-½ cup
- Tomatoes sauce, 1 cup
- Orange juice, 1 cup
- Broth of your choice, 2 cups
- Onion, ½ cup
- Garlic minced, 3 cloves
- Bay leaves, 2
- Crushed fennel seeds and savory leaves
- Salt and pepper (according to taste)

Preparation/Procedure

1. Combine tomatoes, sauce, orange juice, broth, onions, garlic, bay leaves, fennel seeds, and savory leaves in the slow cooker.
2. Cook for 3-4 hours at a high temperature.
3. Add the shrimp at the end (last 15 minutes).
4. Add salt and pepper.
5. Remove bay leaves.
6. Serve hot.

Storage

Cover the container with a lid and store it in the refrigerator.

Reheating

Use the microwave for reheating.

If using a stove, keep the heat at medium.

Nutritional facts/values (per serving)

Calories: 137 | Fat: 1g | Carbohydrates: 9g | Protein: 19g | Sodium: 211mg | Potassium: 331mg | Sugar: 0g

10.2 Slow cooker Fish curry

6 Servings | Preparation time: 10 mins | Cook time: 120 mins

Ingredients/Food list

- Any white fish, 2 cups
- Coconut milk, low fat, 2 cup
- watercress, 1/3 cup
- Onion chopped, 3
- Garlic minced, 3 cloves
- Ginger paste, ½ tsp.
- Thai green curry paste, 2 tbsp.
- Salt and chili (according to taste)

Preparation/Procedure

1. Season the fish with chili and salt. Sauté the onions, ginger paste, and garlic in little oil at a low temperature.
2. Combine fish, the above mixture, coconut milk, and curry paste in the slow cooker.
3. Cook for 2 hours at a low temperature.
4. Check the fish if it's fully cooked.
5. Add the watercress at the end and mix well.
6. Serve hot with rice or noodles.

Storage

Cover the container with a lid and store it in the refrigerator.

Reheating

Use the microwave for reheating.
If using a stove, keep the heat at medium.

Nutritional facts/values (per serving)

Calories: 323| Fat: 9g | Carbohydrates: 9g | Protein: 53g | Sodium: 800mg | Potassium: 0mg | Sugar: 6g

10.3 Slow cooker clam soup

8 Servings | Preparation time: 30 mins | Cook time: 450 mins

Ingredients/Food list

- Diced bacon, 1 cup
- Clams, ¾ cup
- Potatoes diced, 4
- Water with added clam base, 2 cups
- Onion, 1
- Garlic minced, 3 cloves
- Celery, 2 stalks
- Thyme dried, ½ tsp.
- Corn starch, 2 tsp.
- Salt and pepper (according to taste)

Preparation/Procedure

1. In a pan, cook bacon at a high temperature.
2. Combine half the bacon, potatoes, clams, water, onions, garlic, celery, thyme, salt, and chili in the slow cooker.
3. Cook for 7 hours at a low temperature.
4. In a cup, add cornstarch in some water and whisk. Add this mixture to the slow cooker.
5. Cook for 30 minutes at a high temperature.
6. Serve hot with the remaining half bacon.

Storage

Cover the container with a lid and store it in the refrigerator.

Reheating

Use the microwave for reheating.
If using a stove, keep the heat at medium.

Nutritional facts/values (per serving)

Calories: 260 | Fat: 20g | Carbohydrates: 15g | Protein: 19g | Sodium: 530mg | Potassium: 540mg | Sugar: 0g

10.4 Lobsters' consommé

6 Servings | Preparation time: 30 mins | Cook time: 410 mins

Ingredients/Food list

- Lobster tails, 4
- Minced shallots, 2
- Tomatoes diced, 3 cups
- Chicken Broth, 4 cups
- Heavy Cream, 2 cups
- Garlic minced, 1 clove
- Bay leaves, 1 tbsp.
- Salt and pepper (according to taste)

Preparation/Procedure

1. In a pan, sauté shallots in garlic until shallots turn translucent.
2. Add shallots along with broth, tomatoes, bay leaves, salt, and pepper in the slow cooker. Add a fan part of lobsters first in the slow cooker.
3. Cook for 6 hours at a low temperature.
4. Remove the tail ends. Blend the mixture using a blender to make a smooth texture.
5. Now add the lobster tails' meaty parts. Cook for 45 minutes at a low temperature.
6. Remove tails and separate the meat from the shells.
7. Add cream to the slow cooker and stir well. Add lobster meat back.

Storage

Cover the container with a lid and store it in the refrigerator.

Reheating

Use the microwave for reheating.
If using a stove, keep the heat at medium.

Nutritional facts/values (per serving)

Calories: 431 | Fat: 26g | Carbohydrates: 16g | Protein: 19g | Sodium: 1013mg | Potassium: 650mg | Sugar: 1g

10.5 Slow cooker flaky fish

6 Servings | Preparation time: 15 mins | Cook time: 120 mins

Ingredients/Food list

- All-purpose flour, 3 tbsp.
- Butter, 6 tbsp.
- Fish fillets, 3 lbs
- Shredded cheddar cheese, 1 cup
- Milk, 1-½ cup
- Dry mustard, ½ tsp.
- Lemon juice, 1-½ tsp.

- Nutmeg powder, ¼ tsp.
- Salt (according to taste)

Preparation/Procedure
1. In a pan, melt the butter. Stir until smooth after adding the flour, salt, dry mustard, and nutmeg. Allow it to simmer for a few minutes.
2. Add the milk gradually while continuing to whisk until the mixture thickens. Add cheese and lemon juice.
3. Place the fish in the slow cooker and cover it completely with cheese.
4. Cook for 1-1/2 hours at a high temperature.
5. Serve hot with rice.

Storage
Cover the container with a lid and store it in the refrigerator.

Reheating
Use the microwave for reheating.
If using a stove, keep the heat at medium.

Nutritional facts/values (per serving)
Calories: 430 | Fat: 20g | Carbohydrates: 7g | Protein: 50g | Sodium: 912mg | Potassium: 1044mg | Sugar: 0g

10.6 Slow cooker octopus'

4 Servings | Preparation time: 20 mins | Cook time: 300 mins

Ingredients/Food list
- Octopus, 3 cups
- Baby potatoes, 6
- Olive oil, 3 tbsp.
- Capers, 3 tbsp.
- Lemon, 1-½
- Salt and pepper to taste.

Preparation/Procedure
1. Clean the octopus thoroughly and dip the octopus in the boiling water in a pot. Wait until the tentacles curl up.
2. Place the octopus in the slow cooker, add lemon slices, potatoes, salt, and pepper. cover it completely with water.
3. Cook for 5 hours at a high temperature. Drain the water.
4. Thinly slice the octopus and potatoes.
5. Garnish with olive oil, salt, capers, and pepper.

Storage
Cover the container with a lid and store it in the refrigerator.

Reheating
Use the microwave for reheating.

Nutritional facts/values (per serving)
Calories: 406 | Fat: 15g | Carbohydrates: 20g | Protein: 51g | Sodium: 922mg | Potassium: 1141mg | Sugar: 1g

10.7 Jambalaya

8 Servings | Preparation time: 20 mins | Cook time: 300 mins

Ingredients/Food list

- Boneless chicken pieces, 3 cups
- Peeled shrimp, 2 cups
- Chicken broth, ½ cup
- Tomato paste, 1/3 cup
- Tomatoes, diced, 1 can
- Celery diced, 1 cup
- Onions, 2
- Bell pepper, 1
- Cajun seasoning, 2 tsp.
- Minced garlic, 2 tsp.
- Salt and pepper (according to taste)

Preparation/Procedure

1. Combine the chicken, broth, tomato paste, diced tomatoes (with their juices), celery, onions, bell pepper, Cajun spice, garlic, and salt in a slow cooker.
2. Cook uncovered for 4-6 hours at low temperature (or at High temperature for 2 – 3 hours).
3. Take the chicken out of the pot, shred it with two forks, and put it back in.
4. Add the shrimp, cover, and simmer for an additional 10 to 20 minutes, stirring once, or just until the shrimp become pink.
5. Serve with rice.

Storage

Cover the container with a lid and store it in the refrigerator.

Reheating

Use the microwave for reheating.
If using a stove, keep the heat at medium.

Nutritional facts/values (per serving)

Calories: 160 | Fat: 3g | Carbohydrates: 8g | Protein: 24g | Sodium: 861mg | Potassium: 512mg | Sugar: 4g

10.8 Quick Shrimp BBQ

4 Servings | Preparation time: 15 mins | Cook time: 60 mins

Ingredients/Food list

- Peeled shrimp, 1-½ lbs
- Green Onions, 1
- Cajun seasoning, 1 tsp.
- Minced garlic, 2 tsp.
- Butter, ½ cup
- Lemon juice, 1 tbsp.
- Hot pepper sauce, 1 tbsp.
- Salt (according to taste)

Preparation/Procedure

1. In the crock pot, mix the butter, spicy pepper sauce, garlic, Cajun spice, and lemon juice. Add pepper and salt to taste.
2. Cook for 30 minutes at a high temperature.
3. Drain and rinse the shrimp.
4. Pour half of the sauce from the slow cooker into a measuring cup.
5. Put the shrimp in the slow cooker and top with the remaining sauce.
6. Stir to evenly coat.
7. Until shrimp are opaque, cover and simmer at high temperature for 30 minutes.
8. Before serving, top with green onions.
9. For serving, turn to warm.

Storage

Cover the container with a lid and store it in the refrigerator.

Reheating

Use the microwave for reheating.

Nutritional facts/values (per serving)

Calories: 400 | Fat: 25g | Carbohydrates: 7g | Protein: 36g | Sodium: 1580mg | Potassium: 322mg | Sugar: 3g

10.9 Slow cooker steamed Halibut

2 Servings | Preparation time: 5 mins | Cook time: 150 mins

Ingredients/Food list

- Halibut fish, 1- ½ cup
- Lemon juice, 1 tbsp.
- Olive oil, 1 tbsp.
- Dried dill, 1-½ tsp.
- Salt and pepper (according to taste)

Preparation/Procedure

1. In the non-stick foil, put your halibut. Season with salt and pepper.
2. Mix the lemon juice, olive oil, and dill in a small bowl. Over the halibut, drizzle the mixture.
3. Leave lots of space within the foil packet for the fish to steam while you bring up the foil's edges and crimp them together.
4. Place the foil in the slow cooker for 90 minutes at a high temperature.
5. Serve warm.

Storage

Cover the container with a lid and store it in the refrigerator.

Reheating

Use the microwave for reheating.

Nutritional facts/values (per serving)

Calories: 479 | Fat: 6.3g | Carbohydrates: 0g | Protein: 94.4g | Sodium: 339.7mg | Potassium: 2244mg | Sugar: 0g

10.10 Salmon cakes

6 Servings | Preparation time: 30 mins | Cook time: 150 mins

Ingredients/Food list

- Butter, ½ cup
- Cooked salmon flakes, 4 cups
- Marinated artichoke hearts, 6 Oz
- Bay leaves, 1 tsp.
- Minced garlic, 2 cloves
- Breadcrumbs, 1 cup
- Parmesan cheese, ½ cup
- Salt and pepper (according to taste)

Preparation/Procedure

1. Coat the slow cooker with cooking spray.
2. Add butter, garlic, bay leaves, and white vinegar to the slow cooker, and stir the sauce.
3. Place the other ingredients in a bowl and mix them, make patties (cakes), and put them in the refrigerator for 30 minutes.
4. Place the cakes in the sauce. Cover and cook for 1 hour in the slow cooker.
5. Serve when the sauce remains half of its quantity.

Storage

Cover the container with a lid and store it in the refrigerator.

Reheating

Use the microwave for reheating.

Nutritional facts/values (per serving)

Calories: 199 | Fat: 13g | Carbohydrates: 0g | Protein: 15g | Sodium: 111mg | Potassium: 87mg | Sugar: 0g

10.11 Ginger flavored squid

4 Servings | Preparation time: 10 mins | Cook time: 420 mins

Ingredients/Food list

- Squids, 2 cups
- Ginger paste, 2 tbsp.
- Garlic minced, 1 bulb
- Brown sugar, ½ cup
- Soy sauce, ¼ cup
- Oyster sauce, ¼ cup
- Cranberry juice, ¼ cup
- Leeks, 2 stalks
- Bay leaves, 2

Preparation/Procedure

1. Combine the squids, ginger paste, garlic paste, brown sugar, soy sauce, oyster sauce, cranberry juice, leeks, and bay leaves in the slow cooker.
2. Cook for 7 hours at a low temperature.
3. Garnish and serve warm with your favourite dip.

Storage

Cover the container with a lid and store it in the refrigerator.

Reheating

Use the microwave for reheating.

Nutritional facts/values (per serving)

Calories: 208 | Fat: 3g | Carbohydrates: 25g | Protein: 20g | Sodium: 1071mg | Potassium: 390mg | Sugar: 18g

10.12 Fish pie

4 Servings | Preparation time: 10 mins | Cook time: 180 mins

Ingredients/Food list

- Mixed fish, 800g
- Butter, 1/3 cup
- All-purpose flour, 1/3 cup
- Milk, 2 cups
- Fish broth, ½ cup
- Cheddar cheese, ½ cup
- Leek, 1 stalk
- Bay leaf, 1
- Mashed potatoes made with milk and butter (for toppings).

Preparation/Procedure

1. Cook the leeks until softened in a large pot sprayed with oil. Separate it.
2. Bring the butter, flour, and milk to a boil in a saucepan, stirring continually, until thickened and smooth. Add the stock, cheese, and bay leaf.
3. Pour the sauce over the fish in an equal layer in the slow cooker. Cover and cook on low heat for 2-3 hours.
4. Brown in the oven until golden, then top with mashed potatoes and cheese.

Storage

Cover the container with a lid and store it in the refrigerator.

Reheating

Use the microwave for reheating.

Nutritional facts/values (per serving)

Calories: 533 | Fat: 28g | Carbohydrates: 28g | Protein: 42g | Sodium: 1063mg | Potassium: 1140mg | Sugar: 2g

10.13 Cuttlefish

4 Servings | Preparation time: 10 mins | Cook time: 60 mins

Ingredients/Food list

- Cuttlefish fish, cleaned and cut, 1kg
- Olive oil, 5 tbsp.
- Onion, 1
- Garlic minced, 1 clove
- Fresh parsley, a handful
- Cranberry juice, ¼ cup

- Water, 1 cup
- Tomatoes puree, 2 tbsp.
- Salt and pepper

Preparation/Procedure

1. In a skillet, heat extra virgin olive oil, finely chopped onion, smashed garlic, juice and a large sprinkling of sea salt until soft and softly brown in colour.
2. Mix in the finely chopped fresh parsley, sautéed onions, and garlic.
3. Cook for another 2 minutes after adding the cuttlefish.
4. Cuttlefish will begin to become white and leak fluids.
5. Stir in the tomato purée, water, sea salt, and black pepper to mix. Bring to a boil.
6. Reduce the heat to low, partially cover with a lid, and slowly simmer for 45 minutes to 1 hour.
7. Season with sea salt and black pepper to taste.

Storage

Cover the container with a lid and store it in the refrigerator.

Reheating

Use the microwave for reheating.

Nutritional facts/values (per serving)

Calories: 650 | Fat: 12g | Carbohydrates: 10g | Protein: 130g | Sodium: 1121mg | Potassium: 1133mg | Sugar: 8g

10.14 Slow cooker steamed trout

4 Servings | Preparation time: 15 mins | Cook time: 20 mins

Ingredients/Food list

- Trout pieces, 0.8kg
- Lemon, 1
- Olive oil, 2 tbsp.
- Thyme, as needed
- Salt and pepper

Preparation/Procedure

1. Slice the fish or use ready-made steaks. Rinse with water and pat dry with napkins.
2. Combine olive oil, salt, pepper, and lemon juice in a mixing bowl.
3. Leave the fish pieces to soak in the prepared liquid for an hour.
4. Pour a glass of water into a multicooker; it is best to use hot water right away. Thyme sprigs should be thrown.
5. Take out the fish pieces and massage them with the liquid and sauce from the bottom of the saucepan before placing them on a separate plate.
6. Cook for precisely twenty minutes on the "Steaming" program. Remove the tray and serve the fish soon after the signal.

Storage

Cover the container with a lid and store it in the refrigerator.

Reheating

Use the microwave for reheating.

Nutritional facts/values (per serving)

Calories: 241 | Fat: 11g | Carbohydrates: 0g | Protein: 34g | Sodium: 516mg | Potassium: 548mg | Sugar: 0g

11 SIDES AND SMALL PLATES

11.1 Baked potatoes in a slow cooker

4 Servings | Preparation time: 10 mins | Cook time: 4hours 30 mins

Ingredients/Food list
- Potatoes for baking, 4 thoroughly scrubbed
- Extra virgin olive oil, 1 tbsp.
- Salt of kosher to flavor
- Sheets of foil, 4

Preparation/Procedure
1. Potatoes should be forked many times, then rubbed with salt and olive oil. Place in the slow cooker after wrapping tightly with foil.
2. On Low for 7 1/2 hours or on High for 4 1/2 to 5 hours, cook the meat until soft.

Storage
Cover the container with a lid and store it in the refrigerator.

Reheating
Reheat it in the pan or microwave it for 2 minutes.

Nutritional facts/values (per serving)
Calories: 254 | Fat: 4g | Carbohydrates: 51g | Protein: 6g | Sodium: 114mg | Potassium: 1182mg | Sugar: 2g

11.2 Simmering stuffing

16 Servings | Preparation time: 25 mins | Cook time: 4hours 50 mins

Ingredients/Food list
- Butter, 1 mug
- Onion, chopped 2 cups
- Sliced mushrooms,12 ounces
- Chopped celery, 2 cups
- Chopped fresh parsley, 1/4 cup
- Cups of cubed dry bread, 12 cup
- Salt, 1 1/2 teaspoons
- Dried sage, 1 1/2 tablespoons
- Seasoning for poultry, 1 tsp.
- Dried thyme, 1 tbsp.
- Dried marjoram, ½ tsp.
- Black pepper, ground ½ tsp.
- Big, beaten eggs, 2 or as necessary,
- Chicken broth, 4 ½ cups

Preparation/Procedure

1. In a skillet set over medium heat, melt the butter. In butter, cook the onion, celery, mushroom, and parsley for 5 to 8 minutes, stirring occasionally.
2. Bread cubes should be placed in a very big mixing bowl. Over the bread cubes, place cooked vegetables. Add pepper, thyme, marjoram, sage, poultry seasoning, and salt to taste. Mix in the eggs after adding just enough liquid to moisten them. The mixture should be added to a slow cooker.
3. Cook on High with a cover for 45 minutes, then turn the heat down to Low and continue to cook for 4 to 8 hours.

Storage

Cover the container with a lid and store it in the refrigerator.

Reheating

Reheat it in the pan or microwave it for 2 minutes.

Nutritional facts/values (per serving)

Calories: 197 | Fat: 13g | Carbohydrates: 17g | Protein: 4g | Sodium: 502mg | Potassium: 181mg | Sugar: 3g

11.3 Creamed corn prepared slowly

12 Servings | Preparation time: 5 mins | Cook time: 5 hours

Ingredients/Food list

- Frozen corn kernels, 1.4 packages (16 ounces)
- Cream cheese, 1 package (8 ounces)
- Butter, ½ cup
- Milk, ½ cup
- White sugar, salt, and pepper. 1tsp. of each

Preparation/Procedure
1. In a slow cooker, mix corn, cream cheese, butter, milk, and sugar. To taste, add salt and pepper to the food.
2. Cook for 4 to 6 hours on low or 2 to 4 hours on high.

Storage

Cover the container with a lid and store it in the refrigerator.

Reheating

Reheat it in the pan or microwave it for 2 minutes.

Nutritional facts/values (per serving)

Calories: 193 | Fat: 15g | Carbohydrates: 14g | Protein: 3g | Sodium: 114mg | Potassium: 139mg | Sugar: 3g

1.4 Apple butter

32 Servings | Preparation time: 15 mins | Cook time: 10 hours

Ingredients/Food list
- Cored and sliced 1-inch-thick Granny Smith apples, 5 pounds

- White sugar, 1 1/2 cups
- Brown sugar, ½ cup
- Salt, 1tsp.
- Cinnamon powder, 2 tbsp.
- Freshly grated nutmeg, 1/8 teaspoon
- Allspice, ground ½ tsp.
- Cup apple cider vinegar, ¼ cup
- Water splash, 1

Preparation/Procedure

1. Activate the slow cooker and add the apple chunks. Add vinegar, salt, cinnamon, nutmeg, white and brown sugar, as well as vinegar. Mix thoroughly after adding a little water.
2. Cook covered on High for 1 to 2 hours, or until apples begin to soften and release liquid. Cook, uncovered, on Low heat for 5 to 6 hours, or until all the apple flesh is dissolved. Sometimes stir.
3. Until smooth, puree using an immersion blender. Cook for another 4 hours or so, stirring regularly until the mixture has darkened and thickened.
4. If desired, run apple butter through a strainer. Once sealed, place in a glass jar and chill in the fridge.

Storage

Cover the container with a lid and store it in the refrigerator.

Reheating

Reheat it in the pan or microwave it for 2 minutes.

Nutritional facts/values (per serving)

Calories: 82 | Fat: 1.95g | Carbohydrates: 22g | Protein: 0g | Sodium: 75mg | Potassium: 86mg | Sugar: 20g

11.4 Simple Slow Cooker potato cheesiest

10 Servings | Preparation time: 20 mins | Cook time: 2 hours

Ingredients/Food list

- Thawed frozen hash brown potatoes in the South, 2 pounds
- Cheddar cheese, grated into 4 cups.
- Chicken soup cream, 2 condensed cans of 10.75-ounce
- Cream container, 8 ounces
- Finely minced yellow onion, 1 cup(Optional)
- Milk, 1 cup
- Salt for seasoning, or to taste 1 sprinkle
- Garlic mince, 1 tsp.
- Cheese-flavored crackers, 1 cup

Preparation/Procedure

1. In a slow cooker, combine 1/2 cup cheese-flavored crackers, hash brown potatoes, Cheddar cheese, and cream of chicken soup, sour cream, onion, and milk.
2. Cook for about two hours on Low, stirring periodically, until well cooked. Add remaining 1/2 cup of cheese-flavored crackers on top after stirring.

Storage

Cover the container with a lid and store it in the refrigerator.

Reheating

Reheat it in the pan or microwave it for 2 minutes.

Nutritional facts/values (per serving)

Calories: 413 | Fat: 31g | Carbohydrates: 29g | Protein: 17g | Sodium: 826mg | Potassium: 586mg | Sugar: 2g

11.5 Sweet potatoes (yams) with marshmallows cooked slowly

8 Servings | Preparation time: 5 mins | Cook time: 3hours 15 mins

Ingredients/Food list

- Frying oil
- Sweet potatoes, two (29-ounce) cans, drained
- Butter, 1/3 cup diced into 1/4-inch pieces.
- Light brown sugar, ¼ cup
- Little marshmallows, 1 package (16 ounces)

Preparation/Procedure

1. Apply cooking spray to a slow cooker's interior.
2. Sweet potatoes should be placed in a slow cooker with butter on top. Brown sugar should be sprinkled on sweet potatoes.
3. 3 to 3 1/2 hours on high. Cook the marshmallows for about 15 minutes, or until they are soft and somewhat puffy.

Storage

Cover the container with a lid and store it in the refrigerator.

Reheating

Reheat it in the pan or microwave it for 2 minutes.

Nutritional facts/values (per serving)

Calories: 531 | Fat: 8g | Carbohydrates: 109g | Protein: 4g | Sodium: 238mg | Potassium: 663mg | Sugar: 62g

11.6 Oriental White Beans

6 Servings | Preparation time: 10 mins | Cook time: 6hours

Ingredients/Food list

- White kidney beans, soaked in 1 1/2 cups of water overnight
- Tomato paste, 3tsp.
- Red pepper flakes, 1 tbsp.
- Sliced garlic cloves, 3
- Chopped medium onions, 3
- Lemon juice, 1 tsp.
- Cumin, ground 1 tsp.
- Olive oil, two tbsp.
- Pepper and salt as desired
- The beef broth in a single (14.5 ounce) can

Preparation/Procedure

1. Beans, tomato paste, pimento sauce, garlic, onions, cumin, lemon juice, pepper, salt, and extra virgin olive oil, should all be combined in a slow cooker. Mix just enough to coat the beans. Add beef broth, then add just enough water to the top to completely cover the beans.
2. Cook the beans covered for 6 hours on High, or until they are soft and the liquid has thickened. Nothing should be soupy.

Storage

Cover the container with a lid and store it in the refrigerator.

Reheating

Reheat it in the pan or microwave it for 2 minutes.

Nutritional facts/values (per serving)

Calories: 229 | Fat: 5g | Carbohydrates: 37g | Protein: 11g | Sodium: 351mg | Potassium: 848mg | Sugar: 3g

11.7 Sauerkraut in a slow cooker

6 Servings | Preparation time: 15 mins | Cook time: 8hours

Ingredients/Food list

- Drained sauerkraut, 2 pounds
- Bacon fat, 2tbsp.
- Onions, 2 chopped roughly
- Beef broth, 14 ounces
- Complete cloves, 3
- Juniper berries, 4
- Bay leaf, 1
- Caraway seeds, two tsp.
- Salt as desired
- White sugar, one teaspoon, or as desired

Preparation/Procedure

1. In a slow cooker, combine the sauerkraut, bacon grease, and onion. Add the beef broth and season with salt, sugar, caraway seed, bay leaf, cloves, and juniper berries. To blend, stir.
2. Cook for 8 hours on low.

Storage

Cover the container with a lid and store it in the refrigerator.

Reheating

Reheat it in the pan or microwave it for 2 minutes.

Nutritional facts/values (per serving)

Calories: 71 | Fat: 1g | Carbohydrates: 15g | Protein: 3g | Sodium: 1169mg | Potassium: 405mg | Sugar: 6g

11.8 Mushrooms in a slow cooker

4 Servings | Preparation time: 5 mins | Cook time: 3hours 5 mins

Ingredients/Food list
- mushrooms, 1 pound
- butter, 1/2 cups
- envelope of ranch salad dressing mixture, 1

Preparation/Procedure
1. In a slow cooker, combine mushrooms, butter, and ranch salad dressing mix.
2. Cook for three to four hours on low.

Storage
Cover the container with a lid and store it in the refrigerator.

Reheating
Reheat it in the pan or microwave it for 2 minutes.

Nutritional facts/values (per serving)
Calories: 246 | Fat: 23g | Carbohydrates: 7g | Protein: 4g | Sodium: 659mg | Potassium: 403mg | Sugar: 2g

11.9 Yams that are candied over time

6 Servings | Preparation time: 15 mins | Cook time: 3 hours

Ingredients/Food list
- Peeled and quarter-inch-sized yams, 5 cups
- Water, ¾ cup
- Brown sugar, 1 cup
- Pineapple juice, 4 ounces
- Cubed salted butter, ¼ cup
- Vanilla extract, two tbsp.
- Cinnamon powder, 1 tsp.
- A teaspoon of nutmeg, ground ½ tsp.
- Cornflour, two tbsp.
- Water, 2 tbsp.

Preparation/Procedure
1. Cooking spray or a slow cooker liner can be used to cover the interior.
2. Yams should be put in the slow cooker's bottom. Add water, brown sugar, butter, pineapple juice, vanilla, cinnamon, and nutmeg to the top. Stir the sauce to distribute it evenly.
3. Cook for two hours on low. Stir.
4. Make a slurry by mixing cornflour and water in a small bowl. Stir to combine after adding to the slow cooker.
5. About another hour of cooking is required to have the yams fork-tender and the sauce thick.

Storage
Cover the container with a lid and store it in the refrigerator.

Reheating
Reheat it in the pan or microwave it for 2 minutes.

Nutritional facts/values (per serving)

Calories: 396 | Fat: 8g | Carbohydrates: 78g | Protein: 2g | Sodium: 79mg | Potassium: 1121mg | Sugar: 40g

12 POULTRY RECIPES

12.1 The slow cooker chicken with lemon garlic sauce

6 Servings | Preparation time: 15 mins | Cook time: 3hr 15 mins

Ingredients/Food list

- Dried oregano 1 tsp.
- Salt 1/2 tsp.
- Black pepper 1/4 tsp.
- Melted butter 2 tbsp.
- Chicken breast halves, skinless and boneless 2 pounds
- Water 1/4 cup
- Fresh lemon juice 3tbsp.
- Minced garlic cloves, 2
- Granules chicken bouillon, 1tsp.
- Fresh parsley, chopped, 1tsp.

Preparation/Procedure

1. In a small bowl, combine oregano, salt, and pepper. Rub the spice mixture over the chicken breasts.
2. In a pan over medium heat, melt the butter. Cook the chicken in butter for 3 to 5 minutes per side, or until gently browned. Put the chicken in the slow cooker.
3. In the same skillet, combine water, lemon juice, garlic, and bouillon; bring to a boil. Pour over the slow-cooked chicken.
4. Cook on Low for 6 hours or High for 3 hours, covered. 15 to 30 minutes before the slow cooker's cooking time is up, add the parsley.

Storage
Cover the container with a lid and store it in the refrigerator.

Reheating
Reheat it in the pan or microwave it for 2 minutes

Nutritional facts/values (per serving)
Calories: 192 | Fat: 7g | Carbohydrates: 1g | Protein: 30g | Sodium: 348mg | Potassium: 212mg | Sugar: 0g

12.2 Aromatic Slow Cooker Chicken BBQ

6 Servings | Preparation time: 10mins | Cook time: 3hr 10 mins
Ingredients/Food list
- Frozen chicken breast halves, each with no skin or bones, 6 pieces
- Barbecue sauce, 1 bottle (12 ounces)
- Italian salad dressing, 1/2 cup
- Brown sugar, 1/4 cup
- Worcestershire sauce, two tsp.

Preparation/Procedure

1. Chicken should be put in the slow cooker. Pour the mixture over the chicken after combining barbecue sauce, Italian salad dressing, brown sugar, and Worcestershire sauce in a bowl.
2. Cook covered for 6 to 8 hours on low or 3 to 4 hours on high. Slice, then serve.

Storage

Cover the container with a lid and store it in the refrigerator.

Reheating

Reheat it in the pan or microwave it for 2 minutes.

Nutritional facts/values (per serving)

Calories: 300 | Fat: 8g | Carbohydrates: 32g | Protein: 23g | Sodium: 1058mg | Potassium: 331mg | Sugar: 26g

12.3 Chicken in the Slow Cooker with Stuffing

4 Servings | Preparation time: 5 mins | Cook time: 7hr 5 mins

Ingredients/Food list

- Chicken breasts, skinless and boneless, 4 pieces
- Cream of chicken soup for every cup of chicken broth, 10.5 ounce
- The stuffing mixture, 1 box (6 ounces)
- Water, 1/2 cup

Preparation/Procedure

1. In the bottom of a slow cooker, put the chicken. Add broth to the chicken.
2. In a dish, combine the soup, stuffing mix, and water; pour over the chicken.
3. Cook for seven hours on low heat in the slow cooker.

Storage

Cover the container with a lid and store it in the refrigerator.

Reheating

Reheat it in the pan or microwave it for 2 minutes.

Nutritional facts/values (per serving)

Calories: 356 | Fat: 8g | Carbohydrates: 38g | Protein: 30g | Sodium: 1466mg | Potassium: 290mg | Sugar: 4g

12.4 Slow Cooker Cacciatore Chicken

4 Servings | Preparation time: 10 mins | Cook time: 6hr 10 mins

Ingredients/Food list

- Chicken breast halves, each without skin or bones., 4 pieces
- Spaghetti sauce in one jar, 28 ounces
- Tomato paste, 6 ounces
- Fresh mushrooms, sliced, 4 ounces
- Green bell pepper, seeded and chopped, half
- Onion, half minced

- Garlic, minced, 3 tbsp.
- Dried oregano, 1 ½ tablespoon
- Dried basil, ½ tsp.
- Red pepper flakes, ¼ tsp.

Preparation/Procedure

1. In a slow cooker, put the chicken. Add the tomato paste, oregano, basil, black pepper, red pepper flakes, mushrooms, onion, bell pepper, and spaghetti sauce after stirring.
2. Chicken should be cooked on Low for 6 to 8 hours with the cover on.

Storage

Cover the container with a lid and store it in the refrigerator.

Reheating

Reheat it in the pan or microwave it for 2 minutes.

Nutritional facts/values (per serving)

Calories: 364 | Fat: 9g | Carbohydrates: 42g | Protein: 31g | Sodium: 1200mg | Potassium: 1448mg | Sugar: 25g

12.5 Chicken Cordon Bleu Prepared Slowly

6 Servings | Preparation time: 10mins | Cook time: 3hr 10 mins

Ingredients/Food list

- Chicken breast halves, each without skin or bones, 6 pieces
- Condensed cream of chicken soup 10.75 ounce
- Milk,1 cup
- Sliced ham, 4 ounces
- Sliced swiss cheese, 4 ounces
- Dried herbed bread stuffing mix, 8 ounces
- Melted butter, ¼ cup

Preparation/Procedure

1. In a small dish, combine the cream of chicken soup and milk. Fill a slow cooker with enough soup to cover the bottom. Over the sauce, arrange chicken breasts. Swiss cheese is placed on top of the ham pieces. The remaining soup should be poured over the layers while being gently stirred to distribute it.
2. Butter should be drizzled on top of the stuffing before it is sprinkled on. Cook covered for 4 to 6 hours on Low, or 2 to 3 hours on high.

Storage

Cover the container with a lid and store it in the refrigerator.

Reheating

Reheat it in the pan or microwave it for 2 minutes.

Nutritional facts/values (per serving)

Calories: 484| Fat: 21g | Carbohydrates: 35g | Protein: 36g | Sodium: 1206mg | Potassium: 369mg | Sugar: 6g

12.6 Turkey Breast Cooked Slowly

12 Servings | Preparation time: 10 mins | Cook time: 8hours 10 mins

Ingredients/Food list

- Turkey breast, 6 pounds
- Dried onion soup mix, 1 ounce

Preparation/Procedure

1. Rinse and dry the turkey breast. Trim away any extra skin, but save the skin that covers the breast. Spread onion soup mix beneath the skin and all over the exterior of the turkey.
2. Place into a crock pot. One hour on High, covered, followed by seven hours on Low, covered.

Storage

Cover the container with a lid and store it in the refrigerator.

Reheating

Reheat it in the pan or microwave it for 2 minutes.

Nutritional facts/values (per serving)

Calories: 273 | Fat: 2g | Carbohydrates: 2g | Protein: 60g | Sodium: 309mg | Potassium: 577mg | Sugar: 0g

12.7 Chicken Cranberry in a Slow Cooker

4 Servings | Preparation time: 5 mins | Cook time: 4hours 5 mins

Ingredients/Food list

- Chicken breast halves, each without skin or bones, 4 pieces
- Catalina salad dressing, 16 ounces
- Cranberry sauce entire berry 14.5 ounce
- Onion soup mix, 1 packet

Preparation/Procedure

1. In a slow cooker, start by placing the chicken breasts in the bottom. Over the chicken, combine the onion soup mix, cranberry sauce, and salad dressing.
2. Cook for 4 to 6 hours on low.

Storage

Cover the container with a lid and store it in the refrigerator.

Reheating

Reheat it in the pan or microwave it for 2 minutes.

Nutritional facts/values (per serving)

Calories: 740| Fat: 41g | Carbohydrates: 71g | Protein:23 g | Sodium: 1810mg | Potassium: 148mg | Sugar: 50g

12.8 Juicy Slow Cooked Chicken Breast

4 Servings | Preparation time: 10mins | Cook time: 6hours 10 mins

Ingredients/Food list

- Skinless, boneless chicken breast halves weighing, 1 pound
- Small diced tomatoes, 1 (14.5 ounces)
- Chopped onion, ¼ (Optional)
- Seasoning mix, 1 tsp. (Optional)
- Minced garlic clove, 1 (Optional)

Preparation/Procedure

1. In a slow cooker, arrange the chicken. Add onion, garlic, and Italian seasoning after adding tomatoes to the chicken.
2. Cook for 6 to 8 hours on low.

Storage

Cover the container with a lid and store it in the refrigerator.

Reheating

Reheat it in the pan or microwave it for 2 minutes.

Nutritional facts/values (per serving)

Calories: 144 | Fat: 2g | Carbohydrates: 5g | Protein: 23g | Sodium: 208mg | Potassium: 298mg | Sugar: 3g

12.9 Boneless Turkey Breast Cooked Slowly

12 Servings | Preparation time: 10 mins | Cook time: 8hours 10 mins

Ingredients/Food list

- Boneless turkey breast, 10 pounds.
- Dried onion soup mix, 2 packets (1 ounce)
- Water, 1/4 cup
- Garlic powder, 2tsp.
- Powdered onion, 2 tsp.
- Dried parsley, 1/9 cup
- Seasoning salt, 1 tbsp.
- Dried basil, 1 tsp.
- Dried oregano, ¼ cup

Preparation/Procedure

1. The turkey breast should be put in a big slow cooker. Pouring the mixture over the turkey breast and spreading it out to coat the meat evenly after mixing the onion soup mix and water in a basin.
2. To season the turkey breast, put the garlic powder, onion powder, parsley, seasoned salt, basil, and oregano in a bowl and stir until well combined.
3. Cook on Low for 8 to 9 hours, or until the turkey is extremely soft and the spices have given the flesh flavor. The thickest area of the breast should have an instant-read meat thermometer inserted that registers at least 165 degrees F. (75 degrees C).

Storage

Cover the container with a lid and store it in the refrigerator.

Reheating

Reheat it in the pan or microwave it for 2 minutes.

Nutritional facts/values (per serving)

Calories: 468 | Fat: 3g | Carbohydrates: 6g | Protein: 100g | Sodium: 815mg | Potassium: 1011mg | Sugar: 1g

12.10 Turkey Meatballs with Tomato Sauce in a Slow Cooker

6 Servings | Preparation time: 15mins | Cook time: 4hours 5 mins

Ingredients/Food list

- Minced onion, 1/4 cup
- Salad dressing in the Italian style, 1 tbsp.

- Italian-seasoned bread crumbs, 1 ¼
- Cups
- Pounds of ground turkey, 1 ½
- Smashed garlic cloves, 5
- Italian seasoning, 2 teaspoons, of salt, and freshly ground black pepper, to taste
- Chopped tomatoes in the Italian style, 14.5 ounce
- Marinara sauce, one (26-ounce) jar
- Dried basil, 2 tbsp.

Preparation/Procedure

1. In a small sauté pan over medium heat, cook onion and Italian dressing for 5 minutes. Remove from heat and allow it cool for around five minutes.
2. In a bowl, mix the turkey, bread crumbs, garlic, sautéed onions, Italian seasoning, salt, and pepper.
3. In a separate dish, mix the chopped tomatoes, marinara sauce, and dry basil.
4. Layer 1 1/2-inch meatballs made from half of the turkey mixture on the bottom of a slow cooker. Over the meatballs, spread half of the tomato-dice mixture. Layer the remaining tomato mixture on top of the meatballs made with the leftover turkey mixture.
5. Cook covered for 8 hours on low or 4 hours on high.

Storage

Cover the container with a lid and store it in the refrigerator.

Reheating

Reheat it in the pan or microwave it for 2 minutes.

Nutritional facts/values (per serving)

Calories: 415 | Fat: 14g | Carbohydrates: 41g | Protein: 30g | Sodium: 1281mg | Potassium: 888mg | Sugar: 16g

12.11 Legs of Turkey Cooked Slowly

12 Servings | Preparation time: 10mins | Cook time: 7hours 10 mins

Ingredients/Food list

- Turkey thighs, 6 pieces
- Chicken seasoning, 3 tbsp.
- Salt and freshly ground black pepper, as desired
- Aluminium foil, 6 squares of 12x16-inch

Preparation/Procedure

1. The turkey legs should be washed and dried well. Add salt, black pepper, and roughly 1/2 teaspoon of poultry spice to each turkey leg. Wrap the leg with aluminium foil securely. Continue with the remaining legs.
2. In a slow cooker with no liquid or other ingredients, add the wrapped turkey legs. Cook the beef on Low for 7 to 8 hours, or until it is quite soft.

Storage

Cover the container with a lid and store it in the refrigerator.

Reheating

Reheat it in the pan or microwave it for 2 minutes.

Nutritional facts/values (per serving)
Calories: 217 | Fat: 7g | Carbohydrates: 0g | Protein: 36g | Sodium: 102mg | Potassium: 323mg | Sugar: 0g

12.12 Mediterranean Slow Cooker Roasted Turkey

08 Servings | Preparation time: 20 mins | Cook time: 7hours 30 mins

Ingredients/Food list
- Trimmed, boneless turkey breast, 4 pounds with split chicken broth, ½ cup
- Lemon juice, fresh, 2 tsp.
- Pitted kalamata olives, ½ cup
- Finely chopped onion, 2 cups
- Finely sliced oil-packed sun-dried tomatoes, ½ cup
- Seasoning, 1 tsp.
- Freshly ground black pepper, ¼ tsp.
- Salt, ½ tsp.
- Regular flour, 3 tbsp.

Preparation/Procedure
1. In the slow cooker's crock, combine the turkey breast, 1/4 cup chicken stock, lemon juice, onion, kalamata olives, sun-dried tomatoes, Greek seasoning, salt, and pepper. 7 hours on Low with a cover.
2. In a small bowl, mix the flour with the remaining 1/4 cup of chicken broth and whisk to combine. Add to the slow cooker. For an extra 30 minutes, cook on Low with a cover.

Storage
Cover the container with a lid and store it in the refrigerator.

Reheating
Reheat it in the pan or microwave it for 2 minutes.

Nutritional facts/values (per serving)
Calories: 333 | Fat: 5g | Carbohydrates: 9g | Protein: 61g | Sodium: 465mg | Potassium: 755mg | Sugar: 2g

12.13 Turkey Breast with Cranberry Sauce in Slow Cooker

05 Servings | Preparation time: 5 mins | Cook time: 7hours 30 mins
Ingredients/Food list
- Feta cheese, Cut one (3 pounds) into four pieces.
- Water, ½ cup
- Salt, 1/8 tsp.
- Black pepper, 1/8tsp.
- Whole cranberry sauce, 16-ounce

Preparation/Procedure
1. Put the skin-side-up turkey breast in the slow cooker. Add water Turkey breast should be salted and peppered before cranberry sauce is added.
2. About 7 1/2 hours, covered, on Low, until the middle is no longer pink. When implanted close to the bone, an instant-read thermometer should register 165 degrees F. (74 degrees C).

Storage

Cover the container with a lid and store it in the refrigerator.

Reheating

Reheat it in the pan or microwave it for 2 minutes.

Nutritional facts/values (per serving)

Calories: 373 | Fat: 2g | Carbohydrates: 28g | Protein: 59g | Sodium: 168mg | Potassium: 578mg | Sugar: 18g

12.14 Turkey for Thanksgiving Cooked Slowly

12 Servings | Preparation time: 15 mins | Cook time: 8hours

Ingredients/Food list

- Bacon, 5 pieces
- Bone-in skin-free turkey breast, 1 (5 ½ pounds)
- Garlic and pepper, ½ tsp. each
- Turkey gravy, 10.5 ounce
- Regular flour, 2 tbsp.
- Worcestershire sauce, 1 serving
- Dried sage, 1 tbsp.

Preparation/Procedure

1. Over medium-high heat, add the bacon to a pan and cook until it is uniformly browned. Drain, then shred.
2. Cooking spray should be used for slow cooking. Turkey should be placed in the slow cooker. Pepper and garlic for seasoning. Bacon, gravy, flour, Worcestershire sauce, and sage should all be combined in a bowl. Pour on top of the slow-cooked turkey.
3. Cook the turkey for 8 hours on Low in a covered slow cooker.

Storage

Cover the container with a lid and store it in the refrigerator.

Reheating

Reheat it in the pan or microwave it for 2 minutes.

Nutritional facts/values (per serving)

Calories: 382 | Fat: 16g | Carbohydrates: 3g | Protein: 54g | Sodium: 379mg | Potassium: 584mg | Sugar: 0g

12.15 Chicken and Salsa Cooked Slowly

6 Servings | Preparation time: 5 mins | Cook time: 5 hours

Ingredients/Food list

- Sweet onion, cut into rings after being sliced, 1
- Chicken, 1 full (5-pound)
- Salsa, 20-ounce jar

Preparation/Procedure

1. Fill the bottom of a slow cooker with onion rings. Place the breast side of the chicken down on top of the onion layer. Smother the chicken in salsa.
2. Cook for about 5 hours on High, or until the meat is no longer pink at the bone and the juices are clear. 165 degrees Fahrenheit should be displayed on an instant-read thermometer injected into the thickest section of the thigh, close to the bone (74 degrees C).
3. The chicken should be taken out of the slow cooker, covered with two sheets of aluminium foil, and let rest for 10 minutes before being chopped.

Storage

Cover the container with a lid and store it in the refrigerator.

Reheating

Reheat it in the pan or microwave it for 2 minutes.

Nutritional facts/values (per serving)

Calories: 534 | Fat: 28g | Carbohydrates: 8g | Protein: 59g | Sodium: 729mg | Potassium: 765mg | Sugar: 4g

12.16 Slow Cooker Honey Garlic Chicken Thighs

4 Servings | Preparation time: 10 mins | Cook time: 3hours 10 mins

Ingredients/Food list

- Chicken thighs without skin and bones, 4 pieces
- Soy sauce, ½ cup
- Ketchup, ½ cup
- Honey, 1/3 cup
- Minced garlic cloves, 3
- Dried basil, 1 tbsp.

Preparation/Procedure

1. Place chicken thighs in the bottom of a 4-quart slow cooker in a single layer.
2. In a bowl, combine the soy sauce, ketchup, honey, garlic, and basil; pour over the chicken thighs.
3. Cook covered for 6 hours on low or 3–4 hours on high.

Storage

Cover the container with a lid and store it in the refrigerator.

Reheating

Reheat it in the pan or microwave it for 2 minutes.

Nutritional facts/values (per serving)

Calories: 325 | Fat: 12g | Carbohydrates: 34g | Protein: 22g | Sodium: 2204mg | Potassium: 389mg | Sugar: 31g

13 SNACKS AND APPETIZERS

13.1 Sweet corn dip

4 Servings | Preparation time: 15 mins | Cook time: 180 mins

Ingredients/Food list

- Sweet corn, 2 cups
- Jalapeno diced,1
- Cream cheese, 1 cup'
- Parmesan cheese, shredded, ½ cup
- Monterrey jack cheese, shredded, ½ cup
- Garlic powder, ½ tsp.

Preparation/Procedure

1. Add each item to the slow cooker.
2. 2-3 hours on low heat, or until melted.

Storage

Cover the container with a lid and store it in the refrigerator.

Reheating

Use the microwave for reheating.

Nutritional facts/Values (per serving)

Calories: 360 | Fat: 21g | Carbohydrates: 31g | Protein: 15g | Sodium: 535mg | Potassium: 360mg | Sugar: 2g

13.2 Slow Cooker Peanuts

4 Servings | Preparation time: 5 mins | Cook time: 360 mins

Ingredients/Food list

- Peanuts, 1 cup
- Water, 1 quart
- Salt, 2 tbsp.

Preparation/Procedure

1. Put the peanuts in a colander and thoroughly wash them with cold running water to get rid of any dirt or debris.
2. Put the peanuts and water in the slow cooker. Add salt and blend thoroughly.
3. Cook covered for 5 to 6 hours on high, or until desired softness. When cooking, check and, if required, add more water, and stir.

Storage

Cover the container with a lid and store it in the refrigerator.

Reheating

Use the microwave for reheating.

Nutritional facts/Values (per serving)

Calories: 646 | Fat: 32g | Carbohydrates: 31g | Protein: 20g | Sodium: 1096mg | Potassium: 263mg | Sugar: 4g

13.3 Cheese Stuffed Mushroom Chicken Wings

8 Servings | Preparation time: 20 mins | Cook time: 140 mins

Ingredients/Food list

- Parmesan cheese, 1 cup
- Mozzarella cheese, ½ cup
- White mushrooms, 3 cups
- Italian sausage, 1 lb.

Preparation/Procedure

1. Remove stems from mushrooms and clean them.
2. Drain and brown the sausage. Break up into little bits.
3. Combine sausage and mozzarella. Parmesan cheese, 3/4 cup.
4. Stuff each mushroom with the mixture using a spoon and your finger. To fill each mushroom, press the filling.
5. In a greased slow cooker, arrange the mushrooms in a single layer. If more mushrooms are needed, add a second layer, working from the outside in a ring toward the centre.
6. Cook mushrooms on high for approximately an hour, or until they are well heated. Before serving, turn down the heat to maintain warmth and give the flavours another 30 to 60 minutes to meld.
7. Add ¼ cup of parmesan on top for taste.

Storage

Cover the container with a lid and store it in the refrigerator.

Reheating

Use the microwave for reheating.

Nutritional facts/Values (per serving)

Calories: 218 | Fat: 176g | Carbohydrates: 29g | Protein: 125g | Sodium: 4902mg | Potassium: 3432mg | Sugar: 15g

13.4 Chicken Wings

6 Servings | Preparation time: 10 mins | Cook time: 260 mins

Ingredients/Food list

- Chicken wings, 1.5kg
- Corn starch, 2 tbsp.
- Sesame seeds, 1 tbsp.
- Cilantro leaves, 2 tbsp.

For the sauce

- Soy sauce, 1/3 cup
- Vinegar, 1/3 cup
- Brown sugar, 1/3 cup
- Honey, ¼ cup
- Sriracha, 1 tbsp.
- Minced garlic, 3 cloves
- Ginger and onion powder, 1 tsp. each

Preparation/Procedure

1. Combine balsamic vinegar, soy sauce, brown sugar, garlic, honey, Sriracha, pepper, and ginger powder, onion powder in a big bowl and whisk to combine.
2. Put chicken wings in the slow cooker. Add the soy sauce mixture and simmer for 3–4 hours on low heat or 1–2 hours on high heat.
3. Combine cornflour and two tablespoons of water in a small bowl. Mixture into the slow cooker after stirring. For a further 10-15 minutes at high.
4. Broil wings until they are slightly charred and caramelized, on the baking sheet that has been prepared.

Storage

Cover the container with a lid and store it in the refrigerator.

Reheating

Use the microwave for reheating.

Nutritional facts/Values (per serving)

Calories: 160 | Fat: 12g | Carbohydrates: 11g | Protein: 10g | Sodium: 105mg | Potassium: 0mg | Sugar: 0g

13.5 Slow Cooker Lettuce Wraps

4 Servings | Preparation time: 10 mins | Cook time: 10 mins

Ingredients/Food list

- Olive oil, 1 tsp.
- Chicken grounded, 1 lb.
- Minced garlic, 2 cloves

- Onion small, 1 & green onions, 2
- Soy sauce, vinegar, 1 tbsp. of each
- Salt and pepper for taste
- Butter lettuce, 1 head
- Sliced water chestnuts, 1 cup

Preparation/Procedure

1. In a big non-stick pan add up olive oil and chicken ground. Cook and crumble until browned over medium-high heat.
2. Until onions are transparent, approximately 1-2 minutes, stir in ginger, Sriracha, garlic, hoisin sauce, soy sauce, and onion. Chestnuts and green onions should be stirred in until they are soft, about 1-2 minutes; add salt and pepper to taste.

Storage

Cover the container with a lid and store it in the refrigerator.

Reheating

Use the microwave for reheating.

Nutritional facts/values (per serving)

Calories: 376 | Fat: 10g | Carbohydrates: 32g | Protein: 36g | Sodium: 2574mg | Potassium: 658mg | Sugar: 5g

13.6 Grape Jelly-Based Meat Balls

8 Servings | Preparation time: 5 mins | Cook time: 120 mins

Ingredients/Food list

- Grape jelly, 4 cups
- Heinz chili sauce, 3 cups
- Sriracha, 1 tbsp.
- Meatballs, 3 lbs.

Preparation/Procedure

1. With a whisk, combine the grape jelly, chili sauce, and sriracha (if you want it a bit hot) in the slow cooker.
2. 3 pounds of frozen meatballs should be added and stirred into the sauce until evenly coated.
3. Cook on high for two hours or on low for four hours while covering. While serving, keep the setting on "keep warm."

Storage

Cover the container with a lid and store it in the refrigerator.

Reheating

Use the microwave for reheating.

Nutritional facts/Values (per serving)

Calories: 651 | Fat: 37g | Carbohydrates: 94g | Protein: 31g | Sodium: 1312mg | Potassium: 890mg | Sugar: 62g

13.7 Slow Cooker Peach Lactrosse

11 Servings | Preparation time: 20 mins | Cook time: 180 mins

Ingredients/Food list

- Tomatoes, 4 lbs.
- Jalapeño peppers, 4
- Cilantro, ¼ cup
- Onion small, 1
- Brown sugar, ½ cup
- Tomato paste, 1 cup
- Salt and pepper for taste
- Garlic minced, 4 cloves
- Peeled peaches, 4 cups

Preparation/Procedure

1. The first 7 ingredients should be combined in a 5-qt slow cooker before adding 2 cups of peaches. Cook covered on low for three to four hours, or until onion is soft.
2. Add leftover peaches and tomato paste to the slow cooker. Cool.

Storage

Cover the container with a lid and store it in the refrigerator for up to a week or 12 months in the freezer.

Reheating

Thaw at room temperature when using the frozen peach lacrosse.

Nutritional facts/values (per serving)

Calories: 28 | Fat: 0g | Carbohydrates: 32g | Protein: 1g | Sodium: 59mg | Potassium: 15mg | Sugar: 5g

13.8 Slow Cooker Chicken Nachos

6 Servings | Preparation time: 15 mins | Cook time: 480 mins

Ingredients/Food list

- Boneless chicken, 3 lb.
- Olive oil, 1 tbsp.
- Banana pepper rings, 1- ½ cup
- Chicken broth, 2 cups
- Onion small, 1
- Tomatoes chopped, 1 cup
- Monetary cheese, as needed
- Cilantro, Salt, and pepper for taste

Preparation/Procedure

1. Sprinkle salt and pepper on the roast.
2. Seared the roast on both sides in heated oil over high heat.
3. Add roasted chicken, broth, garlic, and banana pepper rings to the slow cooker.
4. For 8 hours simmer at low temperature. Then shred the cooked chicken.
5. Set the oven to 350°. On a baking sheet, spread out the tortilla chips. Top with cheese, tomatoes, onion, black beans, and shredded meat. A ten-minute bake.
6. Serve with avocado, cilantro, and sour cream.

Storage

Cover the container with a lid and store it in the refrigerator.

Reheating

Use the microwave for reheating.

Nutritional facts/Values (per serving)

Calories: 234 | Fat: 4g | Carbohydrates: 39g | Protein: 18g | Sodium: 421mg | Potassium: 120mg | Sugar: 2g

13.9 Slow Cooker Fruit Butter

16 Servings | Preparation time: 30 mins | Cook time: 480 mins

Ingredients/Food list

- Cranberries frozen or fresh, 4 cups
- Ripe pears chopped, 9 cups
- Sugar (granulated), 1-½ cup
- Apple cider vinegar, ½ cup
- Lemon juice, 2 tbsp.
- Grated ginger, 1 tbsp.
- Cinnamon, 1 tsp.
- Salt, ¼ tsp.

Preparation/Procedure

1. In the slow cooker, combine all the ingredients. Around 4 hours on low temperatures. Add mixture to the blender. For approximately a minute, process until smooth. Place in the slow cooker.
2. Turn up the heat to high temperature and cook the mixture for two and a half to three hours, stirring periodically until fully thickened. The mixture should be divided among 16 (4-ounce) jars. Let mixture cool to room temperature for about 2 hours. Bind with jar lids.

Storage

Cover the container with a lid, store it in the refrigerator, or freeze it in the freezer.

Reheating

No need for reheating.

Nutritional facts/values (per serving)

Calories: 215| Fat: 0g | Carbohydrates: 43g | Protein: 4g | Sodium: 594mg | Potassium: 315mg | Sugar: 25g

13.10 Short ribs with tangy sauce

4 Servings | Preparation time: 30 mins | Cook time: 480 mins

Ingredients/Food list

- Short ribs beef, 4
- Olive oil 2 tbsp.
- Onions, 3
- Cornflour mixed in water, 2 tbsp.
- Garlic cloves minced, 4
- Sweet tea, 1 cup
- Beef stock, 1 cup
- Salt and black pepper, ½ tsp.

Preparation/Procedure

1. Short ribs should be seasoned with salt and pepper. Olive oil is heated in a skillet. Add the ribs and simmer for 10 minutes, or until nicely browned. Place in a slow cooker.
2. In a pan, combine the onions, garlic, ginger, and 1/2 teaspoon salt. Cook for 8 to 10 minutes over medium-high heat. Add tea and broth; boil for three minutes. The ribs in the slow cooker with the onion mixture. 7 hours on LOW for cooking.
3. Remove and put aside the ribs. From the slow cooker, strain the ingredients. Reduce liquid in a pan by half by stirring often at medium-high heat. Add salt, sherry vinegar, and add the cornflour mixture by stirring it. 2 to 3 minutes. Eliminate from heat. Pour on ribs.

Storage

Cover the container with a lid, store it in the refrigerator.

Reheating

Reheat in a microwave.

Nutritional facts/Values (per serving)

Calories: 328| Fat: 12g | Carbohydrates: 8g | Protein: 55g | Sodium: 794mg | Potassium: 639mg | Sugar: 4g

13.11 Stuffed bell peppers

6 Servings | Preparation time: 6 mins | Cook time: 45 mins

Ingredients/Food list

- Bell peppers, 6
- White rice, 1 cup
- Chicken broth, 1-½ cup
- Shredded cheese, ½ cup
- Chicken breast cooked, 1 piece
- Seasoning, 2 tsp.
- Salt and pepper

Preparation/Procedure

1. Cut the peppers' tops off, then scoop out the seeds.
2. Instead of using water to cook the rice, use chicken broth. The cheese, cooked chicken, seasoning, salt, and pepper should all be added after the rice has finished cooking.
3. With the rice mixture, stuff each pepper.
4. 45 minutes should be baked after placing on a baking sheet in the slow cooker.

Storage

Cover the container with a lid, store it in the refrigerator.

Reheating

Reheat using microwave.

Nutritional facts/Values (per serving)

Calories: 243| Fat: 0g | Carbohydrates: 66g | Protein: 15g | Sodium: 213mg | Potassium: 344mg | Sugar: 0g

13.12 Butter made from Apples

6 cup Servings | Preparation time: 20 mins | Cook time: 600 mins

Ingredients/Food list

- Apples, 2 lbs.
- Apple cider vinegar, ½ cup
- Sugar 3 cups
- Brown sugar, 1 cup
- Nutmeg powder, 1 tsp

Preparation/Procedure

1. In a slow cooker, combine the vinegar and apple slices.
2. Cook for 6 hours with a cover on, at a high temperature. Add sugars and nutmeg and stir. Reduce the temperature setting to low; cook, covered, for 4 hours. Cool.
3. If desired, strain.

Storage

Cover the container with a lid, store it in the refrigerator for 1 week.

Reheating

No need to reheat.

Nutritional facts/values (per serving)

Calories: 464| Fat: 6g | Carbohydrates: 112g | Protein: 2g | Sodium: 495mg | Potassium: 621mg | Sugar: 88g

13.13 Meatball bites   Quick Mashed Cauliflower

12 Servings | Preparation time: 30 mins | Cook time: 210 mins

Ingredients/Food list

- Cornmeal, 1-¼ cup
- All-purpose flour, ½ cup
- Tomato juice, 5 cups
- Chili powder, 4 tsp.
- Cumin powder, 4 tsp.
- Garlic powder, 2 tsp.
- Salt and pepper
- Spicy pork sausage, 1 lb.

Preparation/Procedure

1. Mix flour, cornmeal, ¾ cup tomato juice, 2 tbsp. chili powder, salt, cumin, garlic powder and pepper.
2. Add sausages and combine well. Make balls.
3. Bake the balls in oven for 20-30 minutes.
4. In the slow cooker, cook remaining tomato juice, cumin powder, chili powder, and salt. Stir the meat balls in it slowly.
5. Cook at low temperature for about 3 hours.
6. Serve hot.

Storage

Cover the container with a lid, store it in the refrigerator.

Reheating

Reheat using microwave.

Nutritional facts/values (per serving)

Calories: 40| Fat: 2g | Carbohydrates: 4g | Protein: 1g | Sodium: 170mg | Potassium: 79mg | Sugar: 1g

13.14 Quick Mashed Cauliflower

6 Servings | Preparation time: 15 mins | Cook time: 210 mins

Ingredients/Food list

- Cauliflower, 1 large head
- Sour cream, full-fat, 1/3 cup
- Garlic, 3 cloves
- Salt and pepper
- Cheddar cheese shredded, 4 Oz

Preparation/Procedure

1. Add 1 inch of water in a slow cooker. Add garlic and cauliflower in it. Set the medium high heat and cook for 7=10 minutes.
2. Drain the water completely.
3. Blend the cauliflower in the blender and then add sour cream. Make it smooth.
4. Add back the puree into the slow cooker, and add cheese. Keep on low temperature to melt the cheese.
5. Add salt and pepper for taste.
6. Serve hot.

Storage

Cover the container with a lid, store it in the refrigerator. Freeze up till 7 months in freezer.

Reheating

Reheat using microwave.

Nutritional facts/values (per serving)

Calories: 130| Fat: 8g | Carbohydrates: 8.4g | Protein: 7g | Sodium: 34mg | Potassium: 18mg | Sugar: 4g

14 DESSERTS

14.1 Slow Cooker Fudge

Servings: 30 | Preparation Time: 15 min | Cook Time: 1 hour

Ingredients/Food List

- Chocolate chips milk 14Oz can
- Sweetened condensed milk 14Oz can
- Vanilla essence 1tsp.
- Unsalted butter ½ Oz

Preparation/Procedure

1. Grease and line an 8x8 pan with baking paper to prepare it. Add each ingredient to the slow cooker.
2. Leave the cover off the slow cooker and set it on low. Stir every 15 to 30 minutes, and cook for one hour.
3. Pour it into the prepared tin when finished.
4. Place for at least two hours in the refrigerator. Cut into squares after setting and enjoy.

Storage

The refrigerator and a sealed container are the ideal places to keep the fudge. Make sure to divide the fudge with some paper if you need to stack it to prevent it from clinging to one another.

Reheating

There is no need to reheat the fudge. Just keep the fudge at room temperature for 2 to 3 minutes and enjoy.

Nutritional Facts/Values (Per Serving)

Calories: 13 | Fat: 6g | Carbohydrate: 17g | Protein: 2g | Sodium: 33mg | Sugar: 16g | Potassium: 68mg

14.2 Chocolate Brownie Pudding

Servings: 6 | Preparation Time: 15 min | Cook Time: 2 hours

Ingredients/Food List

- Boxed brownie mix 18Oz
- Vegetable oil ½ cup
- Large eggs 2
- Water 3 tbsp.
- Milk 2 cup
- Boxed instant chocolate pudding mix 6oz

Preparation/Procedure

1. Spray non-stick cooking spray in a 5 to 6-quart. slow cooker, then keep it aside.
2. Mix the vegetable oil, water, and eggs with the brownie mix in a large bowl until thoroughly incorporated. Fill the slow cooker with batter.
3. Pour the pudding over the brownie mix in the slow cooker after combining the dry instant pudding mix, and 2 cups of milk, whisking them together in a small bowl.
4. For two to three hours, cover and cook on HIGH.
5. Serve warm, either plain or with ice cream or whipped cream.

Storage

Keep the brownie pudding in a container with a lid on it and place it in the refrigerator.

Reheating

Keep the brownie pudding for 10 minutes at room temperature.

Nutritional Facts/Values(Per Serving)

Calories: 647 | Fat: 23g | Carbohydrate: 104g
| Protein: 8g | Sodium: 726mg | Potassium: 304mg | Sugar: 70g

14.3 Slow Cooker Caramel Fondue

Servings: 6 | Preparation Time: 5 min | Cook Time: 1 hour

Ingredients/Food List

- Soft caramels 25
- Mini marshmallows 1/3 cup
- Milk/Heavy cream 1/3 cup
- Flaky sea salt ½ tsp.
- Apple/Strawberries/Bananas for dipping

Preparation/Procedure

1. To the slow cooker, add marshmallows, milk, and caramels.
2. One hour on high in the oven. until smooth, stir. Add salt and stir if required. Take a dip!

Storage

Store the leftover recipe in a container with a lid on it in the refrigerator.

Reheating

There is no need to reheat the caramel fondue, you can eat by keeping it for 10 minutes at room temperature.

Nutritional Facts/Values (Per Serving)

Calories: 30 | Fat: 1g | Carbohydrates: 6g | Protein: 1g | Sodium: 18mg | Sugar: 5g | Potassium: 29mg

14.4 Mixed Fruit Compote

Servings: 18 | Preparation Time: 10 min | Cook Time: 2 hours

Ingredients/Food List

- Sliced peaches 29Oz (2 cans)
- Sliced pear halves 29Oz (2 cans)
- Pineapple chunks 20Oz can
- Sliced apricot halves 15Oz can
- Cherry pie filling 21Oz can

Preparation/Procedure

1. Combine the peaches, pears, pineapple, and apricots in a 5-qt slow cooker. Add pie filling on top.
2. Cook for two hours on high, covered, or until thoroughly heated. Use a slotted spoon before serving.

Storage

Store the leftover dessert in a container with a lid on it and place it in the refrigerator.

Reheating

There is no need to reheat the dessert, you can enjoy it by keeping the dessert at room temperature for 5 minutes only.

Nutritional Facts/Values (Per Serving)

Calories: 190 | Fat: 0g | Carbohydrates: 48g | Protein: 1g | Sodium: 18mg | Sugar: 0g | Potassium: 29mg

14.5 Strawberry Cream Cake

Servings: 6 | Preparation Time: 10 min | Cook Time: 3 hours

Ingredients/Food List

- Strawberry cake mix 15Oz
- Cream cheese 8Oz
- Sugar ¼ cup
- Egg 1
- Vanilla extract 1tsp.
- Cool whip 12Oz for topping

Preparation/Procedure

1. Apply cooking spray to your crock pot.
2. According to the directions on the package, prepare your cake mix.
3. Cream cheese, egg, sugar, and vanilla extract should all be thoroughly combined.
4. Distribute evenly the prepared cake mix in your crock pot.
5. A spoonful of your cream cheese mixture should be dropped onto the batter with a spoon.
6. To make a cream cheese "swirl," cut your batter and cream cheese mixture with a knife.
7. To pass the toothpick test, cook covered on low for 3–4 hours or high for 1–2 hours.
8. Take off your lid and let the cake finish cooling.
9. The cool whips on top

Storage

For up to 7 days, keep in the refrigerator in an airtight jar.

Reheating

It can be kept in an airtight jar for one to two hours at room temperature without needing to be reheated.

Nutritional Facts/Values (Per Serving)

Calories: 213 | Fat: 17g | Carbohydrate: 14g | Protein: 2g | Sodium: 89mg | Sugar: 14g | Potassium: 105mg

14.6 Cinnamon Sugar Candied Almonds

Servings: 4 | Preparation time: 10 mins | Cook time: 4 hours

Ingredients/Food list

- Granulated white sugar 1 and ½ cups
- Brown sugar 1 and ½ cups
- Large egg white 1
- Vanilla extract 2 tsp.
- Raw almonds 4 and ½ cups
- Cinnamon 3tbsp.
- Salt 1/4tsp.
- Water 3tbsp.

Preparation/Procedure

1. Apply non-stick spray to your slow cooker and set it aside.
2. Add the sugar, brown sugar, cinnamon, and salt to a sizable bowl. Blend thoroughly.
3. Add the egg white and vanilla to a different big bowl, and whisk until foamy.
4. Almonds are added to the egg mixture and thoroughly coated by being tossed around.
5. The coated almonds should be poured into the sugar mixture and coated there.
6. Turn the slow cooker to LOW and add the entire mixture.

7. Stirring every 20 minutes, the cooking time will be 3-3.5 hours. For a while, it won't seem like much is happening, but your house will smell great!
8. Add two tablespoons of water and mix thoroughly after three hours. Add one more tablespoon of water if they appear to be dry.
9. Pour the almonds onto the prepared baking sheet when finished, breaking up any that became stuck together. Enjoy after allowing them to gently cool and harden.

Storage

Cover the container with a lid and store it in the refrigerator.

Reheating

Reheat it in the pan or microwave it for 2 minutes.

Nutritional facts/Values (per serving)

Calories: 1553 | Fat: 80g | Carbohydrates: 196g | Protein: 35g | Sodium: 112mg | Potassium: 1282mg | Sugar: 162g

14.7 Pear Cherry Pie Buckle

Servings: 8 | Preparation Time: 10 min | Cook Time: 3 hours

Ingredients/Food List

- Sliced pears 15Oz (2 cans)
- Cherry pie Filling 21Oz can
- Old-fashioned oats ¼ cup
- Almond extract ¼ tsp.
- Yellow cake mix 1 pack
- Melted butter ½ cup
- Sliced almonds ¼ cup
- Brown sugar 1 tbsp.
- Vanilla ice cream (optional)

Preparation/Procedure

1. Pears and pie filling should be combined in a greased 5-qt slow cooker before adding the extract. Cake mix, oats, almonds, and brown sugar are combined in a large basin. Melted butter is then stirred in. sprinkle on top of the fruit.
2. Cook on low, covered, for 3–4 hours, or until the topping is golden. Serve with ice cream, if preferred.

Storage

Cover the container with a lid and store it in the refrigerator.

Reheating

The cake can be eaten by leaving the container at room temperature for a while rather than reheating it.

Nutritional Facts/Values (Per Serving)

Calories: 324 | Fat: 13g | Carbohydrate: 49g | Protein: 1g | Sodium: 152mg | Sugar: 24g | Potassium: 248mg

14.8 Apple Dump Sweet Cake

Servings: 12 | Preparation Time: 5 min | Cook Time: 2 hours

Ingredients/Food List

- Apple pie filling 20Oz (2 cans)
- Yellow cake mix 15Oz can
- Cubed unsalted butter ½ cup
- Ground cinnamon ¼ tsp.

Preparation/Procedure

1. Add both cans of apple pie filling to a slow cooker. To cover the filling, evenly sprinkle cake batter over the top.
2. Sprinkle cinnamon on top of the cake mix after dotting it with butter pieces.
3. For roughly two hours on High, with the lid on, cook the contents until bubbling and the topping until golden.

Storage

The ideal place to keep the cake is a refrigerator. Keep the cake in a container with a lid on it and refrigerate the container.

Reheating

There is no need to reheat the cake. You can have it cold.

Nutritional Facts/Values (Per Serving)

Calories: 319 | Fat: 12g | Carbohydrate: 53g | Protein: 2g | Sodium: 279mg | Potassium: 75mg | Sugar: 26g

14.9 Chocolate Peanut Butter Balls

Servings: 36 balls | Preparation Time: 10 min | Cook Time: 1 hour and 30 min

Ingredients/Food List

- Cocktail peanuts 16oz can
- Chocolate chips 10oz can
- Creamy peanut butter ¾ cup
- Dried cranberries 1 and ½ cups
- Sea salt flakes for garnishing

Preparation/Procedure

1. 2 big rimmed baking sheets should be lined with parchment paper. Place aside.
2. Add peanuts, chocolate chips, and peanut butter to the bottom of a slow cooker. While it is optional, you can whisk the ingredients together if you like. Cook the chocolate on low heat for one to two hours, or until it has melted. Add the lid. View from above a black crockpot with the materials for chocolate-dipped peanut clusters.
3. Dried cranberries are added after the cover is removed. To combine all the ingredients, stir them.
4. Spoon mounds of the melted mixture, each about 1-2 tablespoons high, onto the prepared baking sheets using a tiny scoop. Lightly sprinkling flaky sea salt over the tops. Crockpot peanut butter cluster filling in a cookie scoop.
5. Place in the fridge for a few hours or until solid.

Storage

For up to two weeks, keep in the refrigerator in an airtight container. Possibly frozen for extended storage.

Reheating

Keep the peanut butter balls for 10 minutes at room temperature.

Nutritional Facts/Values (Per Serving)

Calories: 140 | Fat: 10g | Carbohydrate: 13g | Protein: 4g | Sodium: 60mg | Sugar: 7g | Potassium: 108mg

14.10 Banana Foster with Butter

Servings: 4 | Preparation Time: 15 min | Cook Time: 1 hour

Ingredients/Food List

- Butter ½ cup
- Brown Sugar ¼ cup
- Fresh bananas sliced 6
- Rum ¼ cup
- Vanilla ice cream

Preparation/Procedure

1. By setting the slow cooker to Low, melt the margarine. Approximately 10 minutes will pass.
2. When butter or margarine has melted, stir in brown sugar. Add rum and gently mix in the fresh bananas.
3. Cook for one hour on low.
4. Serve the banana mixture with vanilla ice cream.

Storage

Store the banana fosters in a container and place them in the refrigerator.

Reheating

The banana fosters don't require reheating; you can simply consume it after letting it sit at room temperature for 10 minutes.

Nutritional Facts/Values (Per Serving)

Calories: 344 | Fat: 12g | Carbohydrate: 54g | Protein: 2g | Sodium: 139mg | Sugar: 35g | Potassium: 367mg

14.11 Tropical Orange Coconut Cake

Servings: 8 | Preparation Time: 15 min | Cook Time: 4 hours

Ingredients/Food List

- 2% Cold milk 3 cup
- Toasted coconut marshmallows 2 cup
- Coconut cream pudding mix 3.5Oz pack
- Orange cake mix 3.5Oz pack
- Pineapple tidbits 3/4 cup

Preparation/Procedure

1. Whisk milk and pudding mix for 2 minutes in a big bowl. Place in a 5-qt. a slow cooker that has been oiled. Cake mix batter should be prepared by the directions on the package, adding pineapple. Add to the slow cooker.
2. Cook on low, covered, for about 4 hours, or until the cake's edges are golden.
3. Sprinkle marshmallows on the cake after removing the slow cooker insert. Before serving, let the cake sit for 10 minutes, uncovered.

Storage

Cover the container with a lid and store it in the refrigerator.

Reheating

There is no need to reheat the cake, you can consume it by placing the container for some time at room temperature.

Nutritional Facts/Values (Per Serving)

Calories: 518 | Fat: 20g | Carbohydrates: 73g | Protein: 9g | Sodium: 596mg | Sugar: 50mg | Potassium : 674mg

14.12 Cranberry Stuffed Baked Apples

Servings: 4 | Preparation Time: 15 min | Cook Time: 4 hours

Ingredients/Food List

- Large apples 4
- Cranberry Apple drink ½ cup
- Dried cranberries ¼ cup
- Brown sugar 1/3 cup
- Melted butter 2tbsp.
- Cinnamon ½ tsp.
- Nutmeg ¼ tsp.
- Chopped nuts

Preparation/Procedure

1. Apple cores. Apple centres should be filled with cranberries and brown sugar. In a 5- to the 6- quart slow cooker, add the apples.
2. Pour cranberry-apple drink over apples after combining it with butter in a small bowl. Add a dash of nutmeg and cinnamon.
3. Cook for 4 to 6 hours with the cover on a low heat setting.
4. Spoon apples into dessert bowls to serve. Add sauce to the apples. Add some nuts on top.

Storage

Put a lid on the container and keep it in the fridge.

Reheating

Reheat it for two minutes in the microwave or a pan.

Nutritional Facts/Values (Per Serving)

Calories: 290 | Fat: 6g | Carbohydrate: 58g | Protein: 0g | Sodium: 50mg | Potassium: 300mg | Sugar: 49g

14.13 Slow Cooker Caramel Butter-Scotch Cake

Servings: 6 | Preparation Time: 10 min | Cook Time: 2 hours

Ingredients/Food List

- Caramel cake mix 16.5Oz
- Butter 2 tbsp.
- Butterscotch chips 1 cup
- Boiling water 1 and ¾ cups
- Caramel sauce for drizzling

Preparation/Procedure

1. Before cooking the cake, preheat your crockpot by setting it to low for 10 to 15 minutes. Apply nonstick cooking spray to the slow cooker.
2. Melt the stick of butter while reserving 1 cup of the cake mix. Put the remaining cake batter in a sizable bowl.
3. Stir the batter until it is thick and smooth, then add the melted stick of butter and the remaining 1/2 cup of milk. Put the crockpot full of that portion of the cake batter. Spread the mixture evenly around the crockpot's bottom using a spoon.

4. Scatter the butterscotch chips on top of the cake's bottom layer. It's optional, but you may also drizzle about 1/4 cup of caramel over this. Now transfer the 1 cup of cake batter that was set aside to a different medium-sized shallow basin. In the microwave, melt the two tablespoons of butter. In a medium bowl, combine the melted butter and the boiling water. Stir to combine well.

5. Pour the mixture over the cake in the slow cooker, secure the top, and cook for two hours, or until the middle has set. Serve with vanilla ice cream, top with more caramel sauce, and take pleasure in!

Storage

Cover the container with a lid and store it in the refrigerator.

Reheating

The cake can be eaten by leaving the container at room temperature for a while rather than reheating it.

Nutritional Facts/Values (Per Serving)

Calories: 349 | Fat: 17g | Carbohydrates: 50g | Protein: 1g | Sodium: 256mg | Sugar: 42g | Potassium: 76mg

14.14 Oatmeal Chocolate Chip Cookies

Servings: 12 cookies | Preparation Time: 15 min | Cook Time: 3 hours

Ingredients/Food List

- Eggs 2
- Coconut oil ½ cup
- Gluten-free oats 1 and ½ cups
- Powdered sugar ½ cup
- Vanilla 2tsp.
- Grounded flax ½ cup
- Chocolate chips ¾ cup
- Baking powder and salt ½ tsp.

Preparation/procedure

1. Use coconut oil to coat the slow cooker's bottom and sides. Cut a piece of wax paper or parchment paper to fit the slow cooker's bottom. Likewise grease the parchment sheets.

2. Combine coconut oil, eggs, sugar, and vanilla in a medium bowl.

3. The remaining ingredients, minus the chocolate chips, should be combined well in a separate bowl. Mix the wet components with the dry ones. Choco chips should be added until mixed.

4. Smooth the top after spreading the cookie batter into the slow cooker insert.

5. Cook on low for two and a half to three hours.

6. When done, remove the insert from the slow cooker and allow it cool for 30 minutes. Take the parchment paper out of the inset with the cookie dough inside and let it cool for an additional 30 minutes on a wire rack. Cut the cooling mixture into bars.

Storage

Place in an airtight jar and store in the fridge for up to 7 days. For up to three months of storage in the freezer, wrap food in parchment paper and put it in an airtight container or plastic bag.

Reheating

There is no need to reheat it, just keep the air-tight jar for 1 to 2 hours at room temperature.

Nutritional Facts/Values (Per Serving)

Calories: 207 | Fat: 11g | Carbohydrate: 22g | Protein: 4g | Sodium: 130mg | Potassium: 101mg | Sugar: 13g

15 DRINKS

15.1 Slow Cooker Sweet Cider

5 Servings | Preparation time: 10 mins | Cook time: 360 mins

Ingredients/Food list

- Gala or Fuji Apples, 4
- Cinnamon sticks, 2
- Cloves, ½ tsp.
- Allspice, ½ tsp.
- Water, 5 cups
- Brown sugar, ¼ cup

Preparation/Procedure

1. Place apples in the slow cooker. Add cloves, allspice, cinnamon sticks, and 5 cups of water.
2. Cook for 3 hours at a high temperature.
3. Mash the apples with the help of a potato masher, add brown sugar, and for 3 hours at a low temperature.
4. Strain the apple cider and store it.

Storage

Cover the container with a lid, store it in the refrigerator, or freeze it for long-term use.

Reheating

No need to reheat.

Nutritional facts/Values (per serving)

Calories: 122 | Fat: 4 g | Carbohydrates: 32g | Protein: 0g | Sodium: 18mg | Potassium: 181mg | Sugar: 25g

15.2 Ginger based lemonade

12 Servings | Preparation time: 10 mins | Cook time: 360 mins

Ingredients/Food list

- Lemon juice, ¾ cup
- Gingerroot, a 2-inch piece
- Water, 5 cups
- Brown sugar, ¼ cup

Preparation/Procedure

1. Add gingerroot, brown sugar, lemon juice, and 5 cups of water to the slow cooker.
2. Cook for 3 hours at high and 3 hours at low temperatures.
3. Serve hot.

Storage

Cover the container with a lid, store it in the refrigerator, or freeze it for long-term use.

Reheating

No need to reheat.

Nutritional facts/Values (pcr serving)

Calories: 50 | Fat: 0g | Carbohydrates: 13g | Protein: 0g | Sodium: 0mg | Potassium: 0mg | Sugar: 10g

15.3 Orange-honey coffee

12 Servings | Preparation time: 5 mins | Cook time: 120 mins

Ingredients/Food list

- Regular dark coffee, ½ cup
- Orange zest, from ¼ medium orange
- Cinnamon sticks, 2
- Cloves, 8
- Water, 2 quarts
- Honey, ¼ cup

Preparation/Procedure

1. Combine coffee, spices (tie in the cheesecloth bag with orange), and water in the slow cooker.
2. Cook for 2 hours at a low temperature.
3. Add honey at the end and remove the spice bag.
4. Serve when ready.

Storage

Cover the container with a lid, store it in the refrigerator, or freeze it for long-term use.

Reheating

No need to reheat.

Nutritional facts/Values (per serving)

Calories: 37 | Fat: 0g | Carbohydrates: 9g | Protein: 0g | Sodium: 6mg | Potassium: 2mg | Sugar: 20g

15.4 Hot Cocoa

12 Servings | Preparation time: 8 mins | Cook time: 120 mins

Ingredients/Food list

- Brewed coffee, 3 cups
- Cocoa, ½ cup
- Salt, a pinch
- Milk, 5 cups
- Sugar, ½ cup

Preparation/Procedure

1. Combine coffee, cocoa, salt, and sugar in the slow cooker.
2. Add milk to create a smooth texture. whisk the remaining milk slowly. Cook for 2 hours at high temperature.
3. Keep at a warm temperature before serving.

Storage

Cover the container with a lid, store it in the refrigerator, or freeze it for long-term use.

Reheating

Microwave for reheating.

Nutritional facts/Values (per serving)

Calories: 146 | Fat: 6g | Carbohydrates: 18g | Protein: 6g | Sodium: 66mg | Potassium: 15mg | Sugar: 23g

Printed in Great Britain
by Amazon

17274366R00061